America's Haunted Asylums

A Ghost Hunter's Guide

By

Jeff Dwyer

September 1, 2021

Copyright: Jeffrey Dwyer 2021

Publishing by Spirit Publishing
Fairfield, CA

Contact: Jeffreyhdwyer@yahoo.com

ISBN – 9798544954668

Acknowledgement

For invaluable support and inspiration, my thanks go to my colleagues in the paranormal community, especially Loyd Auerbach, Devin Sisk, Ellen MacFarlane, Patti Negri, Norene Balovich, Barry Conrad, Henry San Miguel, Jackie Ganiy, and Carla Heine.

I am especially grateful to Zak Bagans for the opportunity to investigate Alcatraz Prison with him, and appear on *Ghost Adventures*, and discuss my experiences on his TV show, *After Shocks*.

Many thanks to my literary agent, Sue Janet Clark, for helping me learn the vital elements of writing and giving me the support that served as the foundation of my career as a writer.

DEDICATION

This book is dedicated to my friend, Doug Carnahan.

He graciously included me in his paranormal events, stood tall in the paranormal community, befriended many, and gave countless curious souls an opportunity to explore the spiritual aspect of humanity.

Table of Contents

CHAPTER 1

INTRODUCTION TO
GHOST HUNTING IN ASYLUMS

The most haunted places in the world tend to be locations where incarcerated people suffered severe emotional wounds, physical abuse, isolation from compassionate support, and psychological disorders. Foremost among those places are asylums dating from the early nineteenth century to the mid-twentieth century. Few of the persons admitted to these facilities were ever cured of their mental illness. Most lived many years in the fog and misery of mental illness, deprived of access to family members, treatment that might promise a cure, and hope of finding peace and comfort in a troubled life.

For many patients the experience of incarceration was a greater assault on their well-being than the mental illness they suffered. Despite implementation of innovative treatments, the experience of admission to a mental hospital from 1800 to the 1950s was horrific. It is no surprise that patients who died in these places have created the paranormal activity that has been documented by hundreds of investigators.

It is reasonable to ask why the ghost of a person who suffered from mental illness, and the pain and horror of experimental treatments, would remain in the place where they died. This same question has been asked by ghost hunters who investigate battle fields, combat vessels, crashed aircraft, prisoner of war camps, and countless other places filled with the atmosphere of human misery. In the case of mental hospitals, often referred to as asylums, the spirit of a dead patient may remain at the venue because it is not aware that the body is dead. The patient remains in an altered state it does not recognize, awaiting help from a compassionate nurse or doctor, or a treatment that may finally restore a healthy mind. Some patients may be fearful of moving beyond a room or cell which was a place of private refuge, away from treatment rooms and other offending patients. Others may be aware of their death but fearful of moving onward, to the proverbial light or next level of spiritual existence, because they fear judgement or reunion with others who abused them when they were alive. It is likely that some spirits remain in their rooms, or cells, because it was a place of safety - with a warm bed, three meals each day, and medical care - far superior to anything they experienced when alive.

Finally, some spirits may remain in the asylum awaiting an opportunity for revenge against a doctor, nurse, orderly, or guard who abused them physically or caused their death. They may also seek revenge against attorneys who failed to help them avoid incarceration, judges who committed them to the institution, or family members who broke ties due to the mental illness. These may be particularly dangerous spirits that have given several haunted asylums a reputation for frightening experiences reported by many ghost hunters.

Many paranormal experts believe that personality traits, tendencies, and behaviors of criminals and others who suffered from mental illness are not dissipated or resolved by bodily death. It is likely that many retain tendencies for rambunctious, crude, belligerent behavior that may be extreme because they are free of the physical constraints of a physical body. Persons incarcerated in mental institutions due to crimes they committed may remain dangerous as spirits.

Some institutions included in this book had patient populations in which 40% or more of patients were found not guilty of a crime due to insanity. While not specifically found guilty of murder, rape, or other heinous crime, the fact remains that such acts were committed by the patient. Some may be repentant upon the recognition that the bodily has died while others are more angry, belligerent, and dangerous.

Some of the paranormal activity reported in America's haunted asylums cannot be attributed to the presence of the spirit of a dead person. A thickened atmosphere, cold spots, sensation of an unseen being standing close-by, and amorphous or humanoid shadows may be residuals, or *imprints* created by the intense, repetitive emotional experiences of a person while they were alive. Imprints may also include audio phenomena that may such as vocalizations, footsteps, slamming doors, locks turning into place, chains dragging on a stone floor, cracking whips, and noxious odors.

These sounds, odors, and apparent atmospheric anomalies are embedded on the local environment much as electronic analogs are recorded on an audio tape or CD. The clarity, or strength, of the embedded phenomenon depends on the frequency and energy associated with its creation. For example, a sound that is made daily, for many years, such as sobbing under extreme emotional duress, will have high *frequency* and *energy* and become embedded on the electro-magnetic field of the local environment. Often called electronic voice phenomena (EVP) or electronic audio phenomena (EAP), imprints may be perceived by sensitive persons and detected by devices such as infrared cameras and video recorders, and audio recorders.

It is likely that more than 80% of experiences described as *paranormal* may be attributed to imprints rather than ghosts. While the vast majority of "haunted" asylums in the US do harbor ghosts, most of the experiences reported by ghost hunters are perceptions or recordings of imprints. We can say that an encounter with a ghost occurs only when there is a display of intelligent interaction, by a spirit, with the environment or a witness. Intelligent interaction with the environment may include movement of an object, such as turning a door knob, tipping a glass of water, pulling a plug from an electrical socket, causing a rocking chair to move, causing dowsing rods to separate or cross, or pushing a computer off a table. Intelligent interaction with a witness may include a specific answer to a question, perceived through normal hearing mechanisms or captured on an audio recorder. It may also include eye contact with a facial expression of recognition, specific hand gestures, scratch marks on the skin, bruises from contact, and object thrown at the witness.

All of these phenomena – imprints and authentic contact with a ghost – may be experienced at America's haunted asylums. In any case, it is ethical to keep in mind that the experience involves the emotional remnants or spirit activity of persons who suffered from mental illness. Respect and compassion are appropriate together with caution and certain protective measures discussed in Chapters 3 and 25.

BRIEF HISTORY OF ASYLUMS IN THE US

Prior to 1800, most mentally ill persons in the US were sequestered in their home. Confined by a locked door in a basement room or an attic, primitive treatments of starvation, isolation, purging, and blood-letting were common. The first building in America designed specifically for the confinement and treatment of mentally ill persons was constructed in Virginia in 1770. Named the *Public Hospital*, it accepted only patients from wealthy families who suffered from mental illness, and those who were developmentally disabled, who were unable to care for themselves or a danger to others. This hospital is now a museum in colonial Williamsburg. During this period, some general hospitals established separate wards for mentally ill patients. Some hospitals, established by religious groups such as the Quakers of Philadelphia, opened facilities such as the Pennsylvania Hospital with rooms that included shackles attached to the walls.

Early in the nineteenth century a veritable revolution in "asylum medicine" occurred in America. By 1830, the medical profession included physicians who specialized in the treatment of the mentally ill and recognized the specialty of psychiatry, then known as "asylum medicine." New ideas about the treatment of mental illness fostered the rapid growth of insane asylums in most of the larger cities in eastern states. By 1900, more than 300 large psychiatric hospitals had been constructed in the US.

Known colloquially as "nuthouses," or loony bins," and looked upon as disturbing and repulsive places of horror by surrounding communities, many were constructed in elaborate architectural styles with the best electrical, plumbing, heating and cooling systems available. Complete with staff quarters, kitchens, security staff, operating and treatment rooms, offices, and rooms in which visitors could meet with an incarcerated family member, these huge facilities also included a cemetery or burial ground for the remains of patients left unclaimed by family or friends.

Many early practitioners believed that mental illness was the result of environmental factors, primarily tensions the patient experienced in his home or social situation. Doctors believed that over-crowding, poor sanitation, and vice that plagued many cities and towns created most mental disorders. The cure, they believed, was fresh air, security and protection from social tensions, good nutrition, exercise, and productive activity such as working in the hospital's garden.

The transition from a threatening or damaging domestic situation to the compassionate offerings of a large institution was believed to relieve "psychic pain," returning the patient to a rational, productive life. The benefits of many institutions were truly amazing, but the underlying philosophy of early mental institutions was incredibly naïve.

The evolution in asylum medicine in the US was based on ideas imported from Europe that became known as the "moral treatment." This philosophy asserted that mental illness could be cured if the patient was treated kindly in ways perceived by the remaining rational portions of their mind.

Dismissing isolation and harsh restraints, the moral treatment included opportunities for clean air, a safe environment free of threats, meaningful work and recreation, and a system of privileges or rewards for rational behavior.

Recognizing that the design of the hospital was an integral part of the moral treatment, Philadelphia psychiatrist Thomas Kirkbride (1809-1883) devised a plan for construction of mental hospitals that became a template for hundreds of asylums throughout the US. Known as the Kirkbride Plan, this scheme included massive structures that could accommodate a minimum of 250 patients, although many eventually housed more than a thousand. Kirkbride hospitals were large structures with a "narrow, stepped, linear building footprint, often spanning a hundred yards or more. Staggered wings, said to resemble the wings of a bat, that allowed sunlight and fresh air into the wards believed to be an essential element of treatment."

Each wing of a Kirkbride-design hospital functioned separately and included a kitchen, bathroom, infirmary, treatment rooms, and a separate room for each patient with twelve foot high ceilings. A center building, often capped with tall spires or a tower, included apartments for staff and offices.

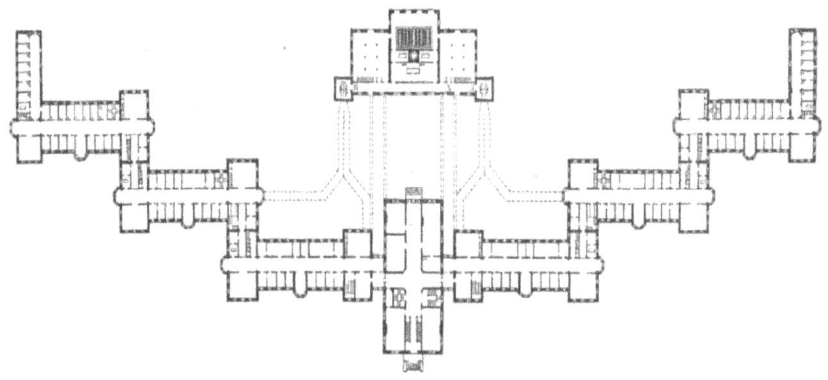

The Kirkbride Plan following a "bat wing" design.

Recognizing that an important element of the moral treatment was outdoor activity, these massive hospitals included a minimum of 100 acres devoted to gardens, farms, recreation areas, and parks. Patients often worked in the farms and gardens, and other supporting industries such as the power plant and water supply system, making the institution self-sufficient.

The first Kirkbride Plan hospital - Trenton State Hospital - opened in Trenton, New Jersey in 1848. By the early twentieth century, the popularity of the Kirkbridge design waned as construction and maintenance costs soared. By 1950 many Kirkbridge structures had been demolished or renovated to such an extent that their original architectural style was undetectable.

Today, thirty Kirkbride buildings remain standing and protected from renovation by registration as national historic places. Examples that may be visited include Trenton State Hospital in Trenton, NJ, Jacksonville State Hospital in Jacksonville, IL, Trans-Allegheny Lunatic Asylum, Weston, WV, Oregon State Hospital, Salem, OR, and Agnews State Hospital in Santa Clara, CA.

Weston State Hospital (Trans-Allegheny Lunatic Asylum), West Virginia.

Despite the philosophy of the *Moral Treatment* and the amenities of Kirkbride hospitals, many asylums were places of horror for patients. Doctors who were not constrained by laws and institutional guidelines for the treatment of patients engaged in experiments that included heinous procedures described later in this chapter. Staff members hired for menial jobs and others not educated or trained in any health care profession abused patients, stole their food, inflicted mental anguish and sometimes committed rape. Unrestrained power and authority granted to the medical director of asylums provided the means to conceal these horrors from government officials and surrounding communities.

By 1950 the concept of massive insane asylums fell out of favor with the psychiatric community. New medications replaced the primitive treatments of the nineteenth century and community mental health systems were established that provided out-patient treatment or short-term stays in small hospitals. Advances in the understanding of brain chemistry and physiology, imaging procedures that have the potential to uncover an organic basis of mental disturbances, distinction between development disability and mental illness, and development of a wide range of medications changed the course of psychiatry and mental health services in the US, leaving the Kirkbridge Plan and its architectural legacy a remnant of history.

HISTORY OF PSYCHIATRIC TREATMENT

Although the Moral Treatment philosophy was the predominant policy in most asylums from 1810 well into the twentieth century, many practitioners experimented with treatment modalities that were, at the very least, torture. In 1887, journalist Nellie Bly was committed to the Blackwell Island Insane Asylum in New York. Upon her release, she reported the inhuman treatment received by a patient with whom she became acquainted. "For crying, the nurses beat me with a broom handle and jumped me. Then, they tied my hands and feet, threw a sheet over my head, and twisted it tightly around my throat so that I could not scream, and thus put me in a bathtub filled with cold water. They held me under until I gave up every hope and became senseless."

Unfortunately, many other forms of treatment inflicted upon patients was far more inhuman.

Isolation, straight-jackets, blindfolds, mouth gags, hoods locked over the head, hand cuffs, leg chains, and ice baths were frequently used in many asylums to subdue patients who spoke loudly, screamed, cried, or moved about their rooms in an uncontrolled manner.

Tranquilizing chair invented by Dr. Benjamin Rush in 1810.

Bloodletting and forced vomiting were used in the belief that mental illness was due to chemical imbalances or excess fluid in the body. Some doctors believed that trephination - opening holes in the skull - would relieve headaches, mental retardation, and release vapors from the brain.

Injection of malaria-infected blood was used to induce fevers believed to cure schizophrenia. Known as Wagner-Jauegg therapy, Doctor Jauegg won the Nobel Prize for Physiology of Medicine in 1927 despite a mortality rate of 15% and lack of proof that the therapy generated any benefit.

In 1927, insulin coma therapy was introduced and remained an often-used treatment modality until the 1960s. With the belief that insulin and blood sugar levels could alter brain function, doctors injected insulin to induce hypoglycemia, or low blood sugar, over long periods of time, sometimes many days. There is no proof that this therapy has any beneficial effect on the mentally ill, but the mortality rate was as high as 10% in some institutions.

In 1938, electro-convulsive shock therapy (ECT) replaced therapies that involved injections of chemical substances and drastic alteration of body fluids. Developed by Italian psychiatrist Ugo Cerletti, seizures in the brain were induced to clear the mind of stray electrical signals believed to be the basis of mental illness. Typically, shocks of 70 to 120 volts were applied for up to six seconds from temple to temple (bilateral ECT) or from front to back of one side of the head (unilateral ECT). ECT is still in use in the US. A

As an alternative to shock therapy, doctors used injections of Metrazol, a trade name for pentylenetetrazol. This powerful CNS stimulant induced convulsions and coma. Despite claims of a success rate of 50% in curing epilepsy and schizophrenia, a high mortality rate led to a decline in its use in the 1940s.

Perhaps the most widely known, and infamous treatment for mental illness is the lobotomy. Originated by Portuguese neurologist António Egas Moniz, the lobotomy involved insertion of a spatula or long spike through the eye socket into the frontal lobes of the brain. The device was then moved about with the intention of severing nerve fibers that connected the lobes to other portions of the brain.

This heinous treatment was introduce in the US in the 1940s by Doctor Walter Freeman who performed more than 3,500 lobotomies before the treatment was abandoned by many psychiatric doctors in favor of antipsychotics, antidepressants, and other medications that proved to be more effective in treating mentally disturbed patients.

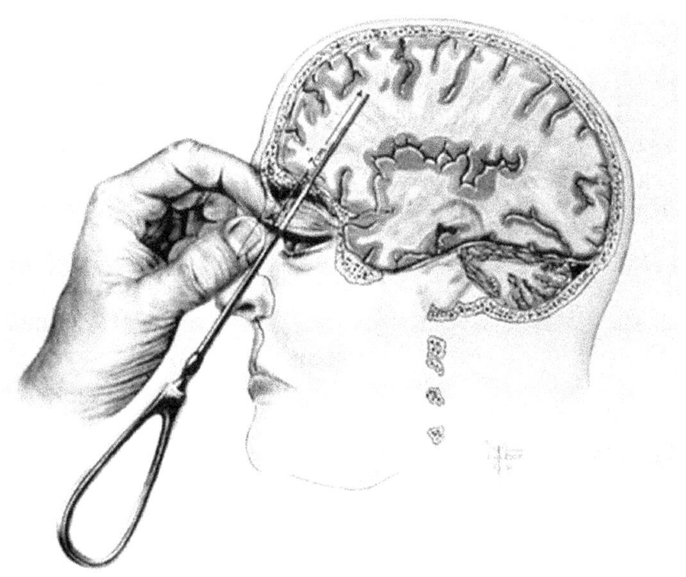

Trans-orbital lobotomy.

By 1960, more than 50,000 lobotomies had been performed in the US with results reported to be "mixed." Most patients were more manageable by hospital staff, but they were left with emotional and intellectual deficits, including memory loss. Few managed to return to responsible work. About 5% of patient died as a result of the procedure while other committed suicide.

NOTABLE PRACTITIONERS

Most medical directors of asylums, staff doctors, nurses, and attendants treated patients with respect and compassion, but there are a few infamous clinicians who may be responsible for thousands of deaths and horrific misery suffered by hundreds of thousands of defenseless patients.

Henry Andrews Cotton (1876–1933) was medical director of New Jersey State Hospital at Trenton (now the Trenton Psychiatric Hospital, previously the New Jersey State Lunatic Asylum) in Trenton, New Jersey from 1907 to 1930. Cotton performed "experimental surgical bacteriology" based on his belief that mental illness was the result of infections in various organs that created toxins that led to neurological dysfunction. His procedure involved removal of some or all of the teeth, tonsils, and, in many cases, the spleen, portions of the intestine, ovaries, and other organs.

Cotton claimed extraordinarily high cure rates that were discredited by medical examiners. When investigated by the New Jersey State Senate, Cotton admitted to death rates as high as 30%, but it is likely that the true death rate was closer to 45%.

Walter J. Freeman MD (1895 – 1972), is best known for introducing into the US the lobotomy as a mainstream treatment for mental. Over a period of four decades, Freeman performed as many as 4,000 lobotomy surgeries in 23 states despite the fact that he had no formal training as a surgeon. Despite claims of success, Freeman's lobotomy left most patients with a variety of neurological deficits including personality changes and memory loss, and emotional disturbances that led to suicide. Official mortalities rate associated with this procedure is 5% but many medical historians believe it was much higher

Benjamin Rush MD (1749-1813) has been dubbed the "Father of American Psychiatry" for many important contributions to the development of mental health asylums in the US, including his seminal book, Medical Inquiries and Observations upon Diseases of the Mind, published in 1812. As a signer of the Declaration of Independence and Treasurer of the US Mint (1799-1813) he was in a position of advocate strongly for the treatment of the mentally ill. Despite this stellar record, he used treatment methods we might view as barbaric. He used bleeding, purging, hot and cold baths, and mercury in his treatments. He invented the tranquilizer chair which confined a patient by wrist and ankle straps and held in place a wooden box that enclosed the head.

Manfred Sakel (1900 – 1957) was a German neurologist who, in 1933, brought the US insulin shock therapy. The treatment modality was comprised of injection of high doses of insulin into patients to trigger convulsions and a coma lasting several hours. After several days of treatment, as many as 60 in some cases, the patient was declared cured. Most patients were left with amnesia and other physiologic disorders. In 1941, 72% of American asylums were using insulin coma therapy for schizophrenia and other mental disorders. Patients who survived the treatments became docile and, thus, appeared to have been cured.

HOW TO USE THIS BOOK

If you are a curious tourist fascinated with dark places that have a paranormal history, you will find this book to be an essential guide to asylums that offer amazing and exciting experiences. Your plans for visiting California, New York, Massachusetts, or West Virginia may be amended to take in the spooky halls of the Trans-Allegheny Lunatic Asylum or the oppressive rooms of the Rolling Hills Asylum in New York. Chapter 2 will provide you with some basic procedures for enticing ghosts to manifest together with methods of capturing evidence of your encounter.

If you are a paranormal enthusiast with some experience hunting ghosts, the hospitals, asylums, and institutions discussed in this book will provide you with specific information about venues where a spectacular encounter with spirits is almost a certainty. With a high probability of a supernatural experience, your skills and knowledge will increase at a fast pace.

If you are an accomplished paranormal investigator, this book will serve as an essential guide to intensely haunted venues that will enhance your resume. Every ghost hunter recognizes the value of broad experiences with spirits that manifest often with high energy. The payoff is a rapidly expanding collection of audio recordings – electronic voice phenomena – infrared still pictures or video, and some fantastic psychic adventures. A resume of investigations that includes

Rancho Los Amigos Hospital in California, Letchworth Village in New York, Waverly Hills Sanatorium in Kentucky, and Western State Asylum in Washington State, is impressive and reflects dedication to the art and science of paranormal investigation.

Chapter two provides a detailed explanation of how ghosts manifest and the best methods for capturing evidence of their interaction with the environment and living persons. Basic and simple technical and psychic methods are presented for the beginner or casual ghost hunters. For the experienced ghost hunter, some advanced technologies and methods and also included.

Chapter 3 – PROTECTION FROM SPIRITS - presents some essential methods of protecting you, the ghost hunter, from troublesome, rambunctious, belligerent spirits and attachments, and other hazards that may be encountered in America's haunted asylums.

*   *   *   *

CHAPTER 2

GHOST HUNTING IN HAUNTED ASYLUMS

Many former asylums are open as museums or historic places and may be visited during regular hours of operation. Your visit a historic asylum may be spontaneous, allowing no time for planning or reading about the history of the institution and some of its better-known events, patients, and staff. In some instances, however, established paranormal investigators who demonstrate a professional attitude and capability, and stipulate a particular reason for an investigation, may be granted special access, including over-night stays. Special access affords weeks to plan an investigation. If this is the case, you should start with research. Summaries of obscure and esoteric material about the venue can be found in museums or obtained from local historical societies.

A few asylums actually have a bookstore that offers published accounts of incarceration and brochures specific to the venue. Local bookstores and libraries usually have special-interest sections with books by local writers. A few inquiries may connect you with these authors, who may be able to help you focus your research.

Participation in a guided tour prior to your investigation of historical sites can help you develop a feel for locations within the facility where ghosts might be sighted. By touring the haunted venue you will have opportunities to speak with guides and docents who may be able to provide you with anecdotes about the dearly departed or tell you ghost stories you can't find in published material. Docents may know people—old-timers in the area, former staff members, or amateur historians—who can give you additional information about specific locations and the potential for ghostly activity.

Almost every city has a local historical society that may have collections that may include photographs, police reports, suicide notes, etc. These are good places to find information that may not be published in mainstream print media. Newspapers are an excellent source of historical information as well. You can search for articles about ghosts, haunted places, or paranormal activity by accessing the newspaper's archives via the Internet and entering key words, dates, or names. Newspaper articles about prison riots, executions, suicides, murders, scandals and suspected or documented paranormal phenomena can provide essential information for your ghost hunt.

TWO BASIC METHODS FOR FINDING GHOSTS

If your visit is spontaneous or initiated with little or no time for preparation and research, the methods you use to experience ghosts and capture evidence of their manifestation should be simple and include minimal instrumentation. An audio recorder, still or video camera, dowsing rods, and a few trigger objects may be more than sufficient and easily transported in a pack-pack or large purse.

If you plan a lengthy, formal investigation during a period of special access, you may want to include more complex instrumentation such as an array of infrared cameras connected to a computer or advanced equipment such as a FLIR mounted on a tripod. This chapter will help you select equipment and methodologies that will enhance your experience.

Some ghost hunters will feel competent with a collection of standard light and infrared cameras, electromagnetic field detectors, digital thermometers, data recorders, and other high-tech gadgets. These ghost hunters prefer to use the *Technical Method.* Others may discover they have an emotional affinity for a particular historic site, a surprising fascination with an event associated with a haunting, or empathy for a deceased person. These ghost hunters may have success with the *Psychic Method.* Another consideration is the ghost hunter's goal. Some desire scientific evidence of ghostly presence while others simply want to experience paranormal activity.

THE TECHNICAL METHOD

Ghost hunters who favor the Technical Method often use an array of detection and recording devices that cover a wide range of the electromagnetic spectrum. Technical methods of ghost hunting can be complicated and expensive and require skilled people to operate the devices. Ghost hunters who want to use the Technical Method yet keep their investigations simple and inexpensive may get satisfying results with common audio and video recording devices and other low-tech approaches.

Equipment Preparation

A few days before your ghost hunt, clear audio and image media of previous recordings. Test your batteries and bring new backup batteries and freshly charged power packs to the investigation site. You should have two types of flashlights: a broad-beam light for moving around a site and a penlight-type flashlight for narrow-field illumination while you make notes or adjust equipment. A red lens will help you avoid disruption of your night-adapted vision

Still-Photography Techniques

Many photographic techniques that work well under normal conditions are inadequate for ghost hunts. Your equipment should include a stable, lightweight tripod. Many cameras have features that enable automatic exposures at specific intervals, e.g., once every minute. This allows a hands-off remote image record to be made. Repetitive automatic exposures also allow a site to be investigated without the presence of the investigator.

While every ghost hunter armed with a camera wishes to capture the full-bodied image of a ghost, most have to settle for light anomalies. These may be amorphous, luminescent clouds or narrow streaks of light resembling a shooting star. The light anomaly most frequently captured in digital images is the orb. An orb is a symmetrical, white disk that appears most often in photographs and digital images made under low-light conditions. It may appear hovering near a ceiling, over a bed, or inside a car. A photograph may contain a single orb or show so many, of varying size, that they cannot be counted. Impressive pictures of light anomalies may be viewed at several Websites.

Many ghost hunters claim that orbs are spirit manifestations without explaining why the spirit of a human would appear as a disk of light. Some of these have a humanoid shape but fail to convince critics and skeptics that the image is that of a ghost because the image is so perfectly illuminated it appears fake. Software for processing digital images has reduced the power of proof that was once attributed to photographs. Critics and skeptics point out that orbs may be the result of bugs, dust particles, or water droplets suspended in the air close to the lens or inside the camera. Excited ghost hunters have displayed pictures of light anomalies that turn out to be the result of wisps of hair, a camera strap, a finger, cigarette smoke, light reflected from jewelry, or smudges on the lens.

Generally, light anomalies should not be readily accepted as evidence of spirit presence unless there is corroborating evidence derived from other technical devices. Corroborating evidence might also be found in psychic impressions experienced at the time and place that the light anomaly was captured. For example, psychic impressions of intense emotions, sobbing and cries for help, or screaming might be obtained while standing in an old hospital room as a photographer captures a picture of an orb hovering over the bed.

Some professional and advanced amateur ghost hunters use infrared photography. Because digital cameras are inherently sensitive to infrared light, minor adjust-ments allow users to take pictures that may reveal entities that would not be seen with conventional photographic techniques. Filters may be purchased that block out visible light while admitting infrared light.

Audio Recording Techniques

Digital recorders provide an inexpensive way to obtain audio evidence of paranormal activity. The popular term for this is "electronic voice phenomena" or EVP. The American Association of EVP defines it as any intelligible voice detected on recording media that has no known explanation. Most ghost hunters accept a wider definition that includes the sound of moving objects, such as doors, windows, or glass objects; whistling; sobbing; laughter; screams; humming; gunshots; footsteps; explosions; musical notes; or tapping and knocking.

Given this wide variety of sounds, I have proposed that the term EVP be replaced by EAP, electronic audio phenomena, and defined as any audio recording that cannot be attributed to normal phenomena. EAP are obtained as a ghost hunter investigates an allegedly haunted place. The ghost hunter may record EAP while remaining stationary at a site, such as within a prison cell or treatment room in an asylum, or while walking around a location. This is called an EAP or EVP sweep. Generally, questions are asked to which spirits may respond. These questions should be simple and follow an invitation for any spirits present to communicate. Typical questions include:

"What is your name?"
"Did you die here?"
"How old are you?"
"Do you want me to leave?"
"Why are you here?"

In most cases, spirit responses cannot be heard by the ghost hunter when they occur but they may be discovered on the audio recording during playback. Typically, responses are brief, rarely lasting more than a few seconds. Vocalizations sometimes have amazing clarity but most often they are unintelligible and, as with other sounds, rarely repeated in subsequent recordings.

Often, EAP consists of non-vocal sounds. Musical instruments, slamming doors, gunshots, footsteps, and tapping sounds may be evoked by the ghost hunter's questions. Ghosts that are unable to generate vocalizations may resort to these sounds as the only means of communication. You may ask, "Why are you here?" On playback, the recording may reveal the sound of footsteps moving away from the microphone. In this instance, the ghost may have been troubled by the question and decided to leave.

Allow time, at least 15 to 60 seconds, for a response. Most EAP can be heard only during playback, so ghost hunters should review recordings every 5-10 minutes during the investigation, rather than waiting until the investigation is completed. This will enable the identification of hot spots for spirit activity that may be investigated more thoroughly.

Remote microphones and monitor earphones allow you to remain some distance from the site and activate the recorder when ghostly sounds are heard. If this equipment is not available, turn the recorder on and let it run throughout your investigation, whether you remain stationary or walk about the site.

Ghost hunters should carefully analyze their audio recordings, and the environment in which they are obtained, to be certain they are not inadvertent recordings of natural or normal sounds. Sound may carry great distances, particularly over bodies of water and when there is fog or low cloud cover. Use software such as Adobe Audition for editing your EAP recording. With practice, you will be able to subdue or eliminate extraneous sounds while enhancing spirit communications.

Video Recording

Video recorders offer a wide variety of recording features from time-lapse to auto-start/stop and autofocus. These features enable you to make surveillance-type recordings over many hours while you are off-site. Consult your user's manual for low-light recording guidelines and always use a tripod and long-duration battery packs.

You may have greater success with sequential recordings, activated manually or by a timer, than a continuous-run technique. If you try this technique, use recording runs of one to five minutes. Practice using the method that interrupts the automatic setting should you need to manually control the recording process.

High-Tech Equipment

You can purchase high-tech devices such as electro-magnetic field detectors, infrared thermometers, barometers, and motion detectors at your local electronics store or over the Internet. Good sources for high-tech ghost-hunting equipment are the Society for Paranormal Investigation, the Ghost Hunter Store, and the EMF Safety Superstore.

Inexpensive, battery-operated motion detectors can be placed at several locations within an investigation site. Some of these allow users to select an audio signal or a silent flashing light signal and connect the output to a central monitor. These devices work by measuring optical or acoustical changes in the environment. Therefore, they are most reliable when remote surveillance is performed and investigators are certain that no living beings have entered the site.

Infrared thermometers have been used to search for cold spots that may signal the presence of a ghost. While these devices are widely utilized, and sometimes displayed on paranormal TV shows, they are often used incorrectly. They cannot assess changes in the temperature of clear air because of its very low density and minimal emission of infrared energy. However, infrared thermometers can detect the surface temperature of solid objects, liquids, dense gases, and clouds.

The most advanced and expensive piece of equipment used by ghost hunters is the FLIR imaging device. FLIR is an acronym for forward-looking infrared. FLIRs detect thermal energy in the infrared range. The FLIR lens focuses the scene on a vast array of sensors that produce thousands of simultaneous measurements of thermal energy. Software then assembles the thermal measurements into a mosaic or picture that is displayed on a handheld video screen. In the picture, elements of the scene are colored according to the temperature or level of infrared radiation. The result resembles a coloring-book image in which some elements are blue, indicating colder temperatures, while others are yellow, orange, or red, indicating warmer temperatures.

FLIR systems can see through atmospheric obscurants such as smoke or fog and in total darkness. Ghost hunters use them to detect spirits that do not generate an image within the human visual spectrum. Theoretically, when spirits appear on our plane they draw energy from the environment, creating a cold spot. A FLIR will detect subtle changes in temperature and depict the shape of the cold spot on the video screen. When the shape of the cold spot is humanoid, ghost hunters claim they have evidence that a ghost is present.

Despite the technical sophistication and expense of FLIRs, the images they produce may be misinterpreted. FLIRs may detect sources of heat or cold created by normal processes not noticed by the user.

Electromagnetic field (EMF) detectors are used by paranormal investigators to detect the presence of ghosts despite the lack of scientific evidence that EMF and spirit presence are linked. Ghost hunters who use EMF detectors claim that spikes in a local electromagnetic field are created when a ghost transitions onto our plane of existence. These devices, however, often pick up EMF generated by unseen electrical appliances, faulty wiring in an old house, cell phones, walkie-talkies, video recorders, electric cars, and numerous other sources including solar flares and geomagnetic storms. EMF detectors may be useful if proper controls are established and all possible sources of natural EMF are identified.

Electronic gadgets can be useful and fun, but unless you have a means of creating a record of the instrument's output or storing images or data in a computer, your reports of light anomalies, apparent paranormal motion of objects, changes in the physical characteristics of the environment, or apparitions will not constitute the kind of hard evidence you need to satisfy skeptics.

Keep in mind that even expensive instruments may produce erroneous data or signals if they are incorrectly calibrated, misused, or improperly maintained. Also, data can be easily misinterpreted if the user does not understand the technical or operating limitations of the device. Using expensive high-tech gadgets does not guarantee accurate results, nor do they validate a ghost hunt as a scientific investigation.

Very Low Tech Devices

Investigators have had great success in detecting spirit activity with common household items. Ghosts often become active when they are irritated by changes in their favored environment. If you tilt a picture hanging on the wall, leave an object in the ghost's favorite chair, or leave a book open, a ghost may straighten the picture, remove the object from his chair, or close the book.

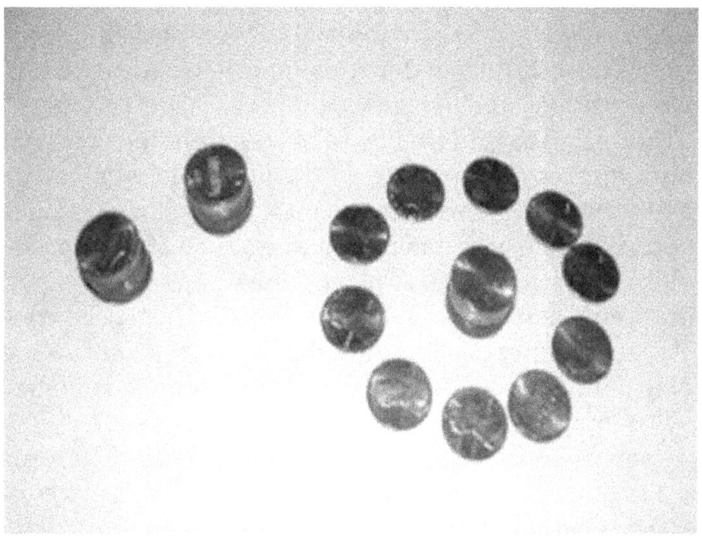

A low-tech trigger object to attract ghosts.

Spirits may be attracted to objects they can manipulate easily. Leave four aces at the top of a deck of cards. A ghost may shuffle them throughout the deck. Ghosts are often attracted to water. A glass left full may later be found empty and the contents wetting the floor. A paper and pencil may be used by a ghost to leave bizarre marks or a legible message. Leave two stacks of coins—10 pennies in each stack—on a stable surface and leave the room for an extended period of time. When you return, the coins may be scattered. If both stacks are scattered, a gust of wind or vibration of the building may account for the change. If one stack remains untouched while the other is scattered, that may be the work of a ghost.

THE PSYCHIC METHOD

The Psychic Method relies upon your intuition, inner vision, or emotional connection with a deceased person, object, place, or point of time in history. You don't have to be a trained psychic to use this approach. All of us have some capacity to tap into unseen dimensions and use some of the psychic tools described in my book *Psychic: Use Your Psychic Powers to Experience Ghosts.* Your ability to use psychic tools for successful ghost hunting depends upon three factors: innate ability, receptivity, and sensitivity.

You may have an ability to successfully use psychic tools in a ghost hunt if you are one of those people who can readily identify isolated places within a room that elicit a chilling feeling that there is something bizarre or paranormal about the spot. The ability to identify these places must include a capacity to sort out your impressions, clear your mind of extraneous thoughts and distractions, and focus your attention on the particular point from which a paranormal impression emanates.

You may have sufficient *receptivity* to effectively use psychic tools if you feel more intensely connected to a place or past era than others or often feel mentally transported to another era. Do you often get that curious feeling that some unseen person is standing behind you, watching you, or touching you? When you touch an artifact, such as a weapon, do you get the impression that you have become aware of information about the object or its user? If so, you are receptive to unseen dimensions and likely to have success hunting ghosts with psychic tools.

You may have exceptional *sensitivity* if you get vivid impressions of emotions in specific locations within allegedly haunted places. Do you walk into a historic building and get that eerie feeling that something or someone from the past still lingers there? Do you get a sense of "vibes" of fear, anger, pain, or suffering when you visit historic places or places known to be haunted? If so, you may be sensitive to residual energies from past events, emotions that played out in a particular place, or the actions of people who have been gone from the scene for decades. Sensitive people often detect a distant time or a voice, sound, touch, or texture of another dimension often described as a change in atmosphere.

Your sensitivity will pay off in a ghost hunt if your investigation is aimed at strong paranormal imprints or attachments of spirits. Strong imprints and attachments are indicated by the frequency, duration, and consistency of the detected paranormal activity that reportedly occurs at a particular place.

The strongest imprints are created by intense emotions such as fear, rage, jealousy, revenge, or loss, especially if they were repetitive over long periods prior to death. Biographical research may reveal this kind of information, particularly if personal letters or diaries are examined. Old newspaper articles, suicide notes, and photographs are useful, too.

You may enhance your sensitivity by developing and expressing empathy for the ghost's lingering presence at a haunted site. Empathy can be based on your research, which may reveal information about the entity's personal history and probable emotions, motivations, problems, or unfinished business at the time of death. You may also learn that a ghost may be trapped, confused, or has chosen to remain at a site to protect someone or guard something precious.

Your sensitivity to ghostly environmental imprints and spirit manifestations may also be increased by meditation, the relaxing of one's physical body to eliminate distracting thoughts and tensions and achieve emotional focus. Meditation allows you to concentrate your spiritual awareness on a single subject—a place, entity, or historic moment in time. Markers of time or season, artifacts or implements, furniture and doorways are a few suggestions of things to focus on.

As the subject comes into focus, you can add information obtained from your research, information that relates specifically to the spirit under investigation such as the type of device used for a suicide or murder, favored book, musical instrument, etc. Through this process, you will become aware of unseen dimensions of the world around you, creating a feeling that you have moved through time to a distant era.

Keep in mind that it is possible to be in a meditative state while appearing quite normal. The process is simple and easy to learn. The variety of meditation methods is broad and beyond the scope of this book. You may locate a meditation methodology online that works well for you but practice it before visiting a haunted location.

Psychic Tools

Clairaudience: The perception of sounds generated by paranormal sources is called clairaudience. The term is derived from the French, meaning "clear hearing." People with this ability may hear the voices of spirits who are trying to communicate or the sounds of events that occurred years or decades earlier. The latter are most often environmental imprints created by intense repetitive emotions or events that had a strong emotional component.

Clairsentience: Some ghosts manifest by creating impressions of physical sensations in receptive people that may include a feeling of being touched. Others are accompanied by fragrances or odors. The ability to perceive or detect these physical sensations and smells that do not truly exist on this plane is called clairsentience. Signature perfumes or the fragrance of favorite flowers can help you identify a ghost. Odors such as cigars, oranges, and hemp are common ghostly manifestations. Sometimes, ghost hunters encounter the noxious odors of rotting meat or burning flesh.

Clairvoyance: Information or impressions may be received from objects or spirits without the use of "normal" senses. The process is called clairvoyance and usually refers to visual impressions. People who see ghosts, whether the image is lifelike or merely a human-shaped fragment of a shadow, are clairvoyant. Visual information or impressions may include orbs, amorphous clouds, or objects. Since clairvoyance is limited to "real time" events, any visual experience suggests a ghost is present at the moment.

Retrocognition: Perception of visual or audio impressions of past events is a form of clairvoyance or clairaudience called retrocognition. Psychic Derek Acorah dramatically portrayed his retrocognition ability during ghost investigations in the popular TV show *Most Haunted.* If you watched my TV shows *Ghosts of the Queen Mary* and *Legends of Alcatraz*, you've seen me perform retrocognition.

Psychometry: Information about an object or one of its users may be obtained by psychically gifted or skilled people through psychometry. First described in 1842 by Joseph R. Buchanan, the process has been used in séances, ghost hunts, and crime scene investigations. After a few minutes of handling an object, practitioners of psychometry get visual impressions or become aware of information that cannot be the result of logical inference (piecing things together from clues you might have).

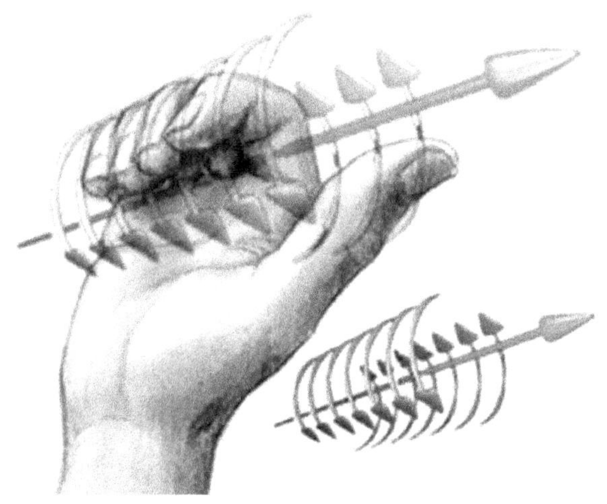

Psychometry: perception of information embedded
in the electromagnetic field of an object.

Ghost hunters can use psychometry to gain information about a spirit's affinity for a chair or a book or why it moves a particular glass or key. Any object that has reportedly been moved by a ghost should be examined by psychometry. Investigators may get clues about the identity of the ghost or reasons for its haunting activity.

Retrieval of information by psychometry may be possible because of changes in an object's electromagnetic field (EMF) created by repetitive handling. Its owner's use may have altered its EMF and left durable traces of the user's energy, much like a fingerprint, especially if intense emotions were associated with frequent use. A good example is my Civil War cavalry saber, which was used in several battles. Psychometrists who handle the saber become aware of fear, rage, and remorse and perceive the image of a middle-aged Union Army officer.

During your visits to prisons, jails, or asylums, perform psychometry by grasping the iron bars with your hands, lay upon the bed once used by an in-mate or patient, and handle artifacts in the site such as a water faucet, metal cup, chair, etc.

SEARCHING FOR GHOSTS

The foremost rule for successful ghost hunting is, be patient! Professional ghost hunters sometimes wait several days, weeks, even months before achieving contact with a ghost. Others have observed full-body apparitions when they least expected it, while concentrating fully on some other activity. Regardless of the depth of your research or preparation, you need to be patient. The serious ghost hunter will anticipate that several trips to a haunted site may be required before some sign of ghostly activity is observed.

If you are ghost hunting with others, it may be advantageous to station members of your group at various places in the ghost's haunting grounds and use a reliable system to alert others to spirit activity. In the event that one member sights a ghost or experiences some evidence of ghostly activity, confirmation by a second person is important in establishing validity and credibility.

Remaining stationary within a cell, treatment room, morgue or other confirmed location is often productive. If a ghost is known to have a favorite chair, bed, or other place within a room, he may manifest there. If your ghost is not known to appear at a specific place within a room or an outdoors area, position yourself to gain the broadest view of the site. A corner of a room is optimal because it allows the ghost unobstructed motion while avoiding the impression of a trap set by uninvited people who occupy his favorite space.

If you are outdoors at an asylum's recreation yard, for instance, position yourself at the corner of the enclosure or in the shadows of a guard tower to conceal your presence while affording a view of your ghost's appearance. If your ghost is a mobile spirit, moving throughout a broad area, you may have no choice but to move around the area. Search for a place where you feel a change in the thickness of the air or a cold spot or detect a peculiar odor.

Once you are on site, the above-described meditation may help you focus and maintain empathy for your ghost. Investigate sounds, even common sounds, as the ghost attempts to communicate with you. Pay attention to your own sensations or perceptions, such as the odd feeling that someone is watching you, standing close by, or touching you. Your ghost may be hunting you!

WHAT TO DO WITH A GHOST

On occasion, professional ghost hunters make contact with a ghost by entering a trance and establishing two-way communications. The ghost hunter's companions hear him or her speak, but the ghost's voice can only be heard by the trance communicator.

In her book, *Adventures of a Psychic*, Sylvia Browne describes several trance communication sessions. Most ghost encounters are brief with little opportunity to engage the entity in con-versation. But the ghost may make gestures or acknowledge your presence through eye contact, a touch on the shoulder, sound, or a movement of an object.

Visitors to historic asylums often feel the touch or tug of a ghost on their arm, hair, or shoulder. In the famous Trans-Allegheny Lunatic Asylum in West Virginia, Philadelphia, ghosts of patients and staff members often give unwary visitors the scare of a lifetime by screaming, touching, slapping, or kicking.

The idea of a close experience with a belligerent or angry ghost is frightening to most of us. More often, the ghost's activities are directed at getting the intruder to leave a cell or other space which may be a sanctuary for the ghost. If you sense your ghost wants you to leave, most hunters believe it is best not to push your luck. When you have established the nature of the ghost activity, ascertained that your companions have experienced the activity, taken a few photographs and run a few minutes of audio, it may be time to leave. An experience with an unfriendly ghost can be disturbing, at the very least.

AFTER THE GHOST HUNT

Turn off all recorders and remove them to a safe place. Some ghost hunters suspect that ghosts can erase recording media. Label your media with the date, time, and location of the ghost hunt. Use a code number for each recording. Keep a separate account of where the recording was made, date, time, and contents. Place media in a waterproof bag with your name, address, telephone number, and a note that guarantees postage in case it is misplaced.

All members of the group should meet right after the hunt, away from the site, for debriefing. Each hunter who witnessed a ghostly activity or apparition should make a written or audio statement describing the experience. Video and audio recordings made at the site should be reviewed and reconciled with witness statements.

*　　*　　*　　*

CHAPTER 3

PROTECTION FROM SPIRITS

The transition from life to death does not cause a spirit become kind, benevolent, or angelic as most people believe. Indeed, spirits do not instantly become aware of vast knowledge about the universe, the true meaning and nature of life, nor can they tap into a storehouse of information and wisdom that is beyond the reach of the living. The erroneous notion that a spirit becomes saint-like fosters the belief that contact with ghosts and other entities cannot be harmful from an emotional, psychological, or physical perspective because the spirit is heavenly and therefore benevolent. Few people realize that this concept is categorically wrong on every level.

It is possible that upon crossing over, or passing through the light to the next higher realm of spiritual existence, an orientation or education process may occur which makes the spirit aware of the wrongs it committed and evil things it may have done when alive and clear the mind of disorders. But most paranormal investigators deal with earth-bound ghosts who have not undergone this evolutionary process. Therefore, you should expect that death has not transformed the entities you seek asylums, including the doctors, nurses and other staff members who may have abused patients.

We should anticipate that defects in their personality and cognition, negative attitudes, and destructive nature persist. These negative traits may even be amplified by the spirit's realization that it is dead and no longer encumbered by a weak or injured body.

Because of negative behavioral traits that may persist within the consciousness of a ghost, we should expect some of them to interact with living persons in ways that are not only frightening and emotionally disturbing, but also psychologically damaging. Therefore, many leaders in the paranormal community believe ghost hunters should use protective measures. The variety of measures used by ghost hunters and demonologists may be classified as physical and psychological.

Before we discuss these protective measures, we need to recognize the dangers of interacting with spirits.

DANGERS OF INTERACTING WITH SPIRITS

Spirits are capable of the same deceptive and emotionally harmful behavior that many of us have encountered with living persons. Beyond that, spirits are also capable of attachment and possession. Many people who are new to paranormal investigation focus mainly on physical hazards because they may have heard stories about people suffering injuries at the hands of ghosts.

The risk of a physical injury is slight, but it is something that should be considered and actively avoided whenever possible.

Physical Hazards: Reports of injuries inflicted by ghosts are rare and their veracity suspect, but many experienced ghost hunters claim to have been scratched, hit, kicked, pushed, and even bitten by ghosts. Leading authorities in the paranormal community believe that rare attacks by ghosts, if they are truly attacks, are a matter of mistaken identity, i.e., the ghost misidentified a living person as a figure the ghost knew during his life. It is possible that encounters interpreted as attacks may be nothing more than clumsy efforts by a ghost to achieve recognition.

Witnesses of life-like ghostly manifestations have found themselves in the middle of gunfights, major military battles, and other violent events, yet sustained not the slightest injury.

Environmental hazards: Investigators may be injured by broken glass, exposed nails, splintered wood, loose floorboards, exposed pipes and wires, low-hanging tree limbs, unstable stairs, and countless other hazards. These hazards may not be seen due to subdued light. For that reason, it is recommended that the venue be visited in daylight hours, or under full illumination, before the investigation is staged.

Hazards can be removed or marked with light-reflecting tape that may be spotted with a low-power flashlight. Environmental hazards are responsible for the vast majority of injuries attributed to ghosts. In many cases, fear or emotional instability may be responsible.

Ghost hunters who lose control of themselves or run when frightened raise the potential for injury.

Lies and Deception: Ghosts may lie especially when questioned about reprehensible behavior they displayed when alive or an embarrassing history of mental illness. Ghosts of mentally ill people are especially prone to confusion, or to misrepresentation as a means of softening our view of them. Ghosts may deceive living persons who seek them by altering their appearance and voice to the extent that an elderly male ghost may appear as a little girl.

Emotional stress: Interaction with angry or malevolent ghosts can lead to emotional stress and fear in the paranormal investigator. Spirits can be overtly frightening, but more often they choose subtle ways of negatively affecting ghost hunters. For instance, instead of slamming doors or scratching your back, a ghost may hover close and make soft, annoying sounds in your ear. '

This kind of thing can be nerve-wracking, especially if it continues for hours or days. Empaths are particularly susceptible to malevolent ghosts who seem to delight in transferring their negative emotions to a living person.

Spirit attachment and possession: There is considerable evidence that a ghost may become attached to a living host, or agent, and move with that person from the venue at which it was discovered. It is likely that many instances of attachment are not malevolent. A ghost may attach to a person known to them or to a stranger if the ghost wants help the host discover a lost object, such as a will or insurance policy. Attachment may also occur when the host invites the spirit to interact with him or her either because of curiosity or a desire to experience the paranormal manifestation of a fascinating character. Some of these may be positive attachments because the ghost's intentions are not destructive and the host is not harmed, although they may be frightened or even emotionally disturbed at times.

Some spirits attach to a host for profoundly negative reasons. An evil spirit may attach because it knew the agent when it was alive. This is especially true if the spirit is motivated by revenge, jealousy, or rivalry. In the vast majority of negative attachments, however, the evil spirit did not know the targeted agent when alive. The spirit may pick on a stranger because it believes it can achieve more control over the agent if it remains anonymous and its operating methods and motivations remain unrecognized or hidden.

Some spirits become more aggressive after death when they realize their new form of existence allows them opportunities to carry-out their manipulative and destructive agenda with far greater ease, unencumbered by the constraints of a physical body.

People who suffer from these negative attachments report the following characteristics of the experience;

1.   The spirit speaks to the host frequently, often through the night disrupting sleep patterns. More than one voice may be heard.

2.   An apparition is rarely seen and movement of objects seldom occurs.

3.   The spirit interrupts the host's thoughts, particularly those aimed at self-assurance that a mentally illness has not begun.

4.   The spirit travels whenever the host travels. These negative, attached spirits are not place-bound. In fact, place has nothing to do with the host-spirit interaction.

Fortunately, these negative attachments are rare, but all ghost hunters should be aware of the dangers and establish safeguards for protection during investigations.

Who is most susceptible to a negative attachment?

1.	People whose energy or spirit is diminished by alcohol or drugs. I advise ghost hunters to never stage an investigation within 12 hours of consuming alcohol and some prescription medications.
2.	People who project or espouse negative thoughts about harmful actions aimed at themselves (suicidal tendencies) or others
3.	Individuals who have a weak grasp on their true self, who are easily manipulated by the living or the dead. These individuals typically waste whatever intellect or skill they may have while pursuing a shiftless, useless life devoid of goals, aspirations, or interest in a career or education.
4.	People who possess exceptional intelligence or rare skills or talent the spirit wishes to use in some way. These may be the most difficult negative attachments to break because spirits feels invigorated by the host's intellect or talent.

Demons: Demons may be the greatest concern of paranormal investigators because of their strength and power. It is suspected that prisons such as Alcatraz and Eastern State Penitentiary house demons, but some authorities refute that assertion. Some investigators - notably the cast of the TV show Paranormal State and members of highly-respected groups such as New England Paranormal Research Society - advise extreme caution when investigators believe they have encountered demon.

Demons have been known to leave an affected person and create a new possession in the body of a well-meaning person who offered help, even members of the clergy.

The vast majority of experienced, professional paranormal investigators are not equipped to deal with this serious problem. Many issues arise that require special knowledge and skill, and possibly licensure as a clinical psychologist or mental health professional, or ordination as a priest. Ghost hunters are advised to refer cases of suspected demonic possession to the few individuals who have the experience, resources, and skills to combat this vicious entity.

Opening portals - Ouija Boards and Séances: Many members of the paranormal community believe that Ouija boards and séances provide opportunities for evil spirits to enter the world of the living and harm anyone in their path. The contrary opinion, held by notable parapsychologists, is that these procedures are not harmful to emotionally stable persons, particularly those who are strong-willed. I might add that people who use physical and psychological measures of protection against spirits typically display the psychic strength to resist the advances of spirits. I've participated in numerous séances and used a Ouija board more than twenty times without negative consequence.

Why do people warn of dangers? I believe it is because some users have mis-interpreted the messages or were psychologically unstable to the extent that they developed irrational fears and psychosomatic disorders such as headaches, sleep disorders, dizziness, etc.

It has been suggested that Ouija boards open a gateway, allowing evil or troublesome spirits to roam the earth. Warnings sometimes mention that Ouija boards may allow evil spirits to enter your home, control your body, or possess people around you. Others advise that, at the very least, the use of a Ouija board is addictive or the information obtained is misleading or misinterpreted. People who are easily impressionable, desperate and irrational thinkers, or gullible, may use Ouija board messages in a way that harms them or people nearby.

The essential question is: can use of a Ouija board enable troublesome or evil spirits "enter" our plane of existence and become attached to us?

Spirits can enter our plane and become attached to us without the use of a Ouija board. The board may facilitate entry of a spirit and attachment just as an audio recorder or any other device that serves as a landing beacon, directing a spirit's attention to a particular individual.

The bottom line, Ouija boards are no different from any other device so they should not be singled out as particularly dangerous.

Séances have the same risks as Ouija boards. Messages may be misunderstood and misinterpreted. Emotionally unstable persons may become upset, anxious, depressed, or even fearful if a message seems in any way threatening. The psychological and physical protective devices described below may not help these people. Therefore, if you, the ghost hunter, stage a séance or use a Ouija board, carefully screen your witnesses and participants for psychological or behavioral traits that may indicate emotional instability or vulnerability to spirit attachment.

All of these hazards can be avoided with a little planning and liberal use of protective procedures and rituals.

PHYSICAL PROTECTION AGAINST SPIRITS

All paranormal investigators, whether their practice is based on the psychic method or technical method, should use protection against angry ghosts and evil spirits to avoid an unwanted attachment or other kinds of harm. Protective measures may not work with demons, but it is wise to perform them anyway.

Physical protection is based on three basic devices that are known to provide some degree of protection: religious icons, Holy water, and herbs. A fourth device – minerals – is sometimes used, as well.

It is important to understand that each device can be used effectively regardless of the user's religious faith, practices, beliefs, or disbeliefs. This is because it is the belief of the evil spirit that matters, not the belief of the living person who seeks protection by using these devices.

Holy Water: The use of Holy water as a sacrament to combat evil spirits, including demons, is a generally believed to be an exclusive rite of the Roman Catholic Church. It is not a ritual that is unique to Catholicism, however. Many religions including Anglicism, Eastern Orthodoxy, and Oriental Orthodoxy use Holy water for baptism, the blessing of persons, places, and special objects, and as a device of protection against or repulsion of evil spirits. In Hinduism and Sikhism, Holy water is used for spiritual cleansing. Islamists use "healing water" to treat spiritual afflictions that may include the effects of evils spirits.

The most common form of Holy water is ordinary tap water that has been blessed by a priest or bishop of the Roman Catholic Church. Protestant churches have Holy water, too, but many paranormal investigators believe that Catholic Holy water is most potent.

Holy water may be used by dipping a finger in the liquid and then drawing the finger across the skin in the sign of the cross, usually on the forehead. This leaves a trace of holy water on the skin, an object that is abhorrent to evil spirits. When done repeatedly, the ritual may result in expulsion of the evil spirit from the affected person or place.

Some practitioners soak a bandana in Holy water and tie it around the head or neck. If you like to keep a room free of evil spirits while you conduct an investigation, wet a finger and leave the moisture in the sign of the cross over every door and window at the location.

When trying to repulse or expel an evil spirit with Holy water it is useful to recite a prayer or invocation that gets the attention of the entity. Again, regardless of the affected person's religious orientation, a tormented person might cross the forehead with Holy water while saying, "By this Holy water, and the precious blood of Jesus Christ, wash away all evil. You are not welcome in this body. You are not welcome in this place."

Protection may be greatest if you drink a tablespoon of Holy before entering the haunted venue. It is interesting to note that most of the information available about Holy water suggests that no additives are used. However, I have one source that says salt should be added when Holy water is used to combat the supernatural.

Religious Icons: Holy water can be more effective if it is used with religious symbols or iconology. The user can carry the icon or place it in a location believed to be occupied by evil spirits. The most potent religious icon is the crucifix. It has been used for centuries to oppose demons and ward off evil including vampires and succubae.

Father Gabriel Amorth, the Roman Catholic Church's foremost exorcist, has stated that the crucifix has great power over demons.

The St. Benedict medal. Left: St. Benedict holds a cross, the object of his devotion, in his right hand and in his left hand he hold the rules for monasteries. Above the cup are the words Crus sancti patris benedicti (The cross of our Holy father Benedict). Surrounding the figure of St. Benedict are the words Eius in obitu nostro prasentia muniamur! (May we be strengthened by his presence in the hour of our death). Right: The reverse side contains the letters C S S M L – N D S M D representing "Crux sacra sit mihi lux! Non draco sit mihi dux!" (May the Holy cross be my light! May the dragon never be my overlord!). Surrounding the back of the medal are the letters V R S N S M V – S M Q L I V B representing Vade retro santana! Nunquam suade mihi vana! Sunt mala quae libras. Ipse venena bibas! (Be gone Satan! Never tempt me with your vanities! What you offer me is evil. Drink the poison yourself!). Finally, located at the top is the word PAX meaning peace.

Herbs: It has been known for centuries that burning sage in a place tends to drive away rambunctious or evil spirits. Sage is only one of many herbs believed to be irritating to evil spirits.

Others include ague weed, agrimony, dill, heather, lavender, pine, and garlic. These herbs can be carried in a plastic bag on your person or in your equipment bag. Some of them can be burned and used for smudging rituals.

Non-religious icons may have power over evil spirits depending upon numerous factors including the spirit's recognition of the device and the past history with those who have used it. These icons include a bell or wind chime, a violet candle, various gemstones, incense, salt, brass, silver, magical charms and hag stones.

Many believe the Saint Benedict Medal has similar power because inscribed on the backside are letters representing Jesus' admonition "Step back, Satan." St. Benedict medals can be carried on your person, in your equipment bag, placed in your car, or placed within a site tormented by evil spirits.

Protection: It is easy to create a small bag that can be carried during paranormal investigations that may confer protection against evil spirits. A sandwich-sized baggie or leather pouch may be filled with a few sprigs of sage and lavender, a St. Benedict medal, a crucifix, hag stones, and small vial of Holy water.

PSYCHIC PROTECTION AGAINST SPIRITS

Current perspectives on what we might call psychic protection against spirits are based to a great extent on the work of British psychoanalyst Violet Mary Firth (1890-1946). In 1930, Firth published Psychic Self-Defense, under the pen name Dion Fortune, in which she described techniques for establishing defenses against the psychic attacks staged by living persons. Widely read by followers of both the British and American Spiritualist Movements, the techniques were later applied to spirits. The basic tenant of Firth's work is to combat a psychic attack with psychological processes. Over the past seven decades, various interpretations and modifications of this tenant have been described as a protective process based on emotional energy and visualization.

The concept of visualization is well-developed by Michelle Belanger in her seminal book The Ghost Hunter's Survival Guide. Noting that spirits manifest through manipulation of energy, she advises us to respond in kind. That is, we must respond by generating our own psychic energy in a way that creates a psychic shield. Like many psychics, Belanger also emphasizes the importance of grounding and centering when faced with the potential for encounters with negative spirits. We will discuss these concepts in the following pages together with my view that we must also project our psychic energy to ward off psychic attack. Each step requires extensive visualization and, for that reason I recommend that meditation precede each procedure to insure mental and emotional clarity.

Effective protection against harmful spirits and the energy of imprints may be created by working within yourself psychologically using a four-step methodology.

The first step is aimed at creating a shield which most spirits cannot penetrate. We don't have to create something new, but merely rejuvenate and strengthen our existing shield, described by many experts as the aura. The aura is a layer of emotional and spiritual energy that extends a few inches beyond the physical boundaries of our bodies. Kirlian photography has produced some amazing pictures of human auras.

Surrounding the entire body, the aura is the true representation our "personal space." We don't often think of it as a kind of shield, but when others invade this space we almost always feel the intrusion. Some sensitive people may actually feel violated. We may feel these things even if the objectionable person does not physically enter our aura.

The negative feelings we experience are the result of the psychic penetration of the aura, usually through weak points. Spirits can do the same thing. Once they penetrate the aura, they can form unwanted and unpleasant attachments. Spirits are particularly good at finding weak points -- cracks in the aura or places where it is very thin – because they are entirely psychic entities and the aura is a psychic phenomenon.

The aura can be strengthened by increasing its thickness and energy content. Thick, high energy auras are impenetrable to even the most belligerent spirits. Methods of strengthening the aura have been beautifully described by Shirley MacLaine in her book, Going Within: A Guide for Inner Transformation. In the context of protection against ghosts, we could use the following process;

1.   Start with meditation to eliminate internal and external distractions and reduce extremes of energy fluctuation.
2.   Turn your psychic vision inward and find the ball of yellow light that exists at the Solar Plexus chakra. Notice that the ball spins. Cause the ball to spin faster, radiating the light outward in all directions.
3.   Visualize or psychically "see" the light moving outward in a uniform fashion, illuminating the skin.
4.   With minimal effort, keep the ball spinning and project the light beyond the skin, joining with your aura.
5.   Visualize the light creating a uniform thickness all over your body while you increase the brightness by expanding the ball at your solar plexus.
6.   Visually smooth the surface of your rejuvenated aura while you brighten the light and radiate it evenly in every direction from the surface of your body.
7.   Some experts advise that, upon attaining this condition, we speak an affirmation. Belanger recommends: "I am surrounded on all sides by light. No darkness shall pass this boundary."
8.   Periodically, brighten your aura by stepping away from the investigation or séance and repeating steps 1 through 6.

In addition to strengthening the aura as a shield against spirits, there may be some instances when we must be proactive. That means we may need to project shielding energy to an object, such as a bloody axe used to kill an entire family or a jail cell in which a mass murderer died, to deflect the energy imprints and attached spirits from launching an attack. We can do this by proceeding through steps 1 through 8 outlined above and then adding a ninth step.

Step nine is the projection of aura energy to a specific object or place through intense visualization. This process requires us to eliminate all distractions, rev up psychic energy, and visualize energy moving through space to the target object. Essentially, we must achieve the same energy state that a poltergeist agent attains but without the emotional or mental disturbance. By contacting the object with your energy, you may effectively freeze or neutralize negative energy that may radiate from it toward you.

If you are unable to create an adequate shield before coming into contact with a negative energy from an object or nearby spirit, you will have to eliminate it from your person psychically. This can be done through grounding and centering. Grounding is the process of elimination while centering is the process of restoring your energy balance after you are free of the assault.

Grounding is most useful when we feel we have been psychically pushed off balance and into a state of dis-coordination by chaotic energy. This can happen any time, even when you are not investigating a haunted place or attempting to perceive spirits. It may happen when you walk into a hospital to visit a friend. It may happen while you play in a park constructed over a former Indian burial ground.

Since the event is psychic, we must deal with it psychically using visualization. We must use the analogy of a lightning rod, channeling or directing electricity through a structure and then harmlessly into the ground.

Follow these steps:

1. Quickly but effectively meditate
2. Take three slow, relaxed cleansing breaths
3. Focus your psychic vision inward and see a dark ball. This is negative energy that has assaulted you.
4. Continue slow and relaxed breathing. With each exhalation, push the dark ball lower in your body, eventually pushing it to your feet.
5. Continue to push the dark ball downward into the ground. As it moves out of your body, fill the space it once occupied with your own bright light.

Belanger advises us that we should immediately follow this process with centering. This is simply a restoration of the psychic energy within our physical body and aura. After pushing a dark ball of negative energy out, we may still feel out of balance. This indicates that we must center ourselves by restoring the equilibrium of our energy. We can do this by simply returning to that central ball of yellow light at the solar plexus and proceeding through steps 2 through 6 that I presented in the section on shielding. Spin the ball of light, increase its energy, and visualize the resulting light moving outward to the entire surface of your body. The key here is to recognize places where the light is a little dim or the energy is a little low. These are the places you must "fill in" with your psychic energy. The process is completed when you feel liberated from distracting, disturbing spiritual energy.

*   *   *   *

CHAPTER 4

INSANITY BY THE BAY

Ghosts of the Insane Asylum
Western State Hospital
9601 Steilacoom Boulevard
Lakewood 98498-7213
253-582-8900

This asylum was established in Washington Territory in 1871, nearly twenty years before statehood was granted. Known as Insane Asylum of Washington Territory, patients and staff were housed in small buildings originally constructed for military use between 1849 and 1868. After only four years of operation, the territorial government took control of the asylum due to several complaints about patient neglect, brutal abuse, and poor living conditions. In 1875, the state legislature renamed the place *Hospital for the Insane in the Washington Territory* to emphasize that the mission of the facility was hospital-based treatment of mental illness, not incarceration and isolation from society. Dr. John W. Waughop served as superintendent from 1880 to 1887 and expanded the facility, its services, and bed capacity, and over-saw development of farms, shops, and other facilities.

The original buildings of the creepy asylum were demolished in 1886 to make way for a massive 4-story structure. Renamed Western Washington Hospital for the Insane, and the main ward was completed in 1887 and, within a few years, the patient population quickly grew to two hundred. In each of the following decades numerous out-buildings were constructed.

From 1876 to 1952, patients who died on the premises were buried in graves marked only with a small stone engraved with a number. Only a few traditional headstones were placed that contained the names of the deceased. Official records indicate that 2,777 graves were placed there. (There may be as many as 3,200 graves, many of which are unmarked.) Most graves contain cremated remains.

The names of those buried remain a secret that cannot be penetrated by the Freedom of Information Act. The fact that the deceased were mentally ill is the basis of their continued anonymity and may be the basis of the high frequency of ghostly activity at the graveyard and nearby barn where some headstones are kept.

The Western State Hospital cemetery is located on the opposite side of Steilacoom Boulevard SW from the hospital campus. Take Angle Lane SW about a quarter of a mile, and then turn right onto Dresden Lane SW. Go one hundred feet, turn onto a gravel road and find the gate to the cemetery. A pyramid-shaped monument stands inside the gate.

A local group of paranormal investigators known as AGHOST (Amateur ghost hunters of Seattle Tacoma) has staged ghost hunts in the cemetery that yielded interesting results. Some sensitives and psychics in the group detected the presence of several spirits who did not realize they were dead wandering the graveyard. This may be the result of their mental illness, mental deficiencies, or simply a lack of pre-death connection with the body that allows a post-death recognition of the body's death.

One member of AGHOST encountered the spirit of a 35-year old man who was unhappy with his stay at the hospital and complaining that no one would give him a razor for shaving. Ghost hunters have captured orbs on film, and in digital images, and encountered mists appear when climatic conditions do not generate fog throughout the grounds. These isolated cells of mist are called ectoplasm. Also, electro-magnetic field detectors have identified several hot spots or technical "hits."

Cemetery ghosts are looking for their bodies or some information about their identities when they were alive. After death, they may have gained a "normal" mental status or, at least, sufficient mental function to understand their new existence and to discover they have questions about their lives and how they died. Ghost hunters who use a psychic approach may find this a useful tact when they try to contact these ghosts.

Across Dresden Lane SW from the cemetery, look for the log barn where displaced headstones are stored. The barn is the venue for an annual event staged in October to generate support for the cemetery and commemorate those buried anonymously on the grounds.

One of Western State's better-known patients was actress Frances Farmer (1913-1970). In 1942, after a series of traffic violations, drunken brawls in Los Angeles bars, aberrant behavior in the courtroom, and arrest by police that involved dragging the actress from her hotel room, naked, Farmer was admitted to the psychiatric ward of Los Angeles General Hospital on January 20, 1943. There, she was diagnosed with manic depressive psychosis. Within two weeks, she was transferred to a minimum-security psychiatric institute where she was diagnosed with paranoid schizophrenia and treated with insulin-shock therapy. In her autobiography Framer claims she was given this treatment for 90 consecutive days.

In September of 1943, Farmer moved to her parents' home in West Seattle and again displayed violent behavior. Her mother had her committed to Western State Hospital, but she was discharged three months later and declared "completely cured." In May of 1945, Farmer was recommitted to Western State where she remained for five years in the high-security ward for the hospital's most violent patients.

In a 1958 interview, she stated: "It was very much like anyone else's that is admitted to a public institution. They don't have means for individual psychiatric care, there's only so many beds available. I stood in line with 15 or 20 girls like myself, in the hospital for one reason or another. We received shots, or hydrotherapy baths, or electric shock treatment. This was supposed to relax the tensions and keep us quiet, which it did. I don't blame the hospital at all—I think that they did everything in their power to take care of the enormous number of people they had, but I really don't think it helped me much."

In later interviews, and her autobiography, Farmer described inhuman treatment and abuse that included being forced to eat her own feces, serve as a sex slave for male doctors and orderlies, suffer rape, eat spoiled food, chained in a padded cell, confined by a straight jacket, and immersed in ice baths. She also claimed she had undergone trans-orbital lobotomy although many of the hospital's staff denied that occurred. Hospital records support the claims of doctors and nurses that Farmer did not have a lobotomy.

In 1982, Jessica Lange portrayed Farmer in the feature film *Frances* which she undergoes a lobotomy. The portrayal of this treatment will interest ghost hunters.

Closed, abandoned, or renovated to other use, mental health facilities are good places to hunt ghosts. Naturally, facilities that currently treat patients – such as Western State Hospital - are not generally accessible to the public unless they feature a museum or specific buildings to commemorate their history. Ghost hunters should not enter patient treatment area without explicit permission.

*   *   *   *

CHAPTER 5

COMMUNITY OF MISERY

Fairview Hospital and Training Center
2250 Strong Road SE
Salem 97310-0540
503-986-5050

The creepiest place in Oregon may be the Fairview Training Center in Salem. Unfortunately for ghost hunters, it may also be the most inaccessible place since the grounds are closed to visitors and ominous signs warn those who consider trespassing that they may face a speedy prosecution.

It is possible, however, to get a good look at this place and even feel some of the negative energy that remains there by approaching the broken fences or the single strands of chain that are intended to keep visitors out. To many ghost hunters, the history of this place and fascinating reports of paranormal activity posted by reliable investigators create a strong attraction to those who want to have an intense ghostly encounter.

Construction of this large collection of buildings, tunnels, wells, and farm facilities was begun in1907 when the State of Oregon created the Oregon Institution for the Feeble-Minded. Late in 1908 the first 39 residents were transferred from the Oregon State Insane Asylum. Standing on 670 acres, the center had plenty of land for gardens, orchards, a dairy, and small farm animals that provided stabilizing and instructional activity for inmates while enabling the place to be nearly self-sufficient in food production. By 1911, the inmate population was 181 with 25 on a waiting list for admission.

In 1917, the State's commitment law was changed and Fairview was no longer permitted to admit people who were legally declared insane. Inmates were described as "feeble-minded" but the community also included those with epilepsy and mental retardation. Elimination of an age minimum in 1921, allowing admission of infants, caused the population to rise from 389 to about 950 by 1928. In addition, admission was now open to orphans, hitchhikers, promiscuous girls, mongoloids, and drug abusers.

A few years later, community sensitivities had changed prompting a change in the facility's name to the Oregon Fairview Home in 1933. Throughout WWII the home's population continued to soar, reaching a peak number if 1,235 inmates in 1948. In 1965, the name was changed again to Fairview Hospital and Training Center. Finally, in 1979, it was known simply as Fairview Training Center.

On February 24, 2000, the last resident left Fairview Training Center, ending a ninety-two year period of attempted altruism, medical treatment, and social experiments which, unfortunately, also included isolation of children who should have remained with their families. Treatment also included physical and emotional abuse, forced sterilizations, "time out" in cages, ice baths, and the liberal use of straitjackets, handcuffs, forced feedings, leg shackles, and psychotropic drugs. It isn't any wonder that numerous escape attempts occurred and an untold number of children and young adults died here. The official list of inmates who died at Fairview is short compared to the number of patients who simply disappeared from the roster of residents.

It is known that, in 1970, two boys drowned in a small lake used by Fairview inmates for swimming and fishing. A cemetery once existed on the grounds of Fairview but some historians believe several unofficial burial sites were filled between 1920 and 1950.

Abandoned building at Fairview Training Center.

After Fairview's closure, a few former residents and staff members gave interviews to newspapers and TV news outlets, or posted reports on the Internet about strange events they experienced in the residential units, common rooms, and the maze of underground tunnels that connect several buildings. Many of those reports created a reputation that the place was a site of intense paranormal activity. Given this esoteric history, it shouldn't surprise anyone that intense paranormal activity occurs in many of the buildings and grounds of Fairview.

Despite mental incapacitation, it likely that many residents were horrified to find themselves incarcerated there. Furthermore, many of them probably missed their family and the support of relatives. After death, it might be anticipated that residents would wait at Fairview for the day when a parent would arrive to take them home.

Other spirits, having been given up by their parents might remain there because they feel they have nowhere to go. Still, others may be angry about forced sterilizations or other physical abuse and they are waiting for revenge on doctors and staff members.

Hollie Pollock may continue to haunt the cistern near Fairview's Withcombe Cottage because he is deeply distraught over the mutilation of his body. In November of 1923, Hollie was found to be missing when roll call was taken. It was immediately assumed he had escaped from the facility since escape attempts were common. A few weeks later, pieces of skin and hair emerged from water pipes as staff members filled tubs for washing clothes. Someone suspected contamination of the cistern by a dead animal. When the cistern was opened, the remains of Hollie's body were found. The paranormal activity at the site is said to be so intense that cars parked close by often fail to start. Others claim to hear a voice calling out from the now-covered cistern.

A Fairview doctor recounted his experience with a young male resident who had suffered an epileptic seizure. At the time, the resident was alone, but he was quickly discovered by a woman who rushed to the adjacent building and alerted medical staff. After aid was quickly rendered and the patient as stabilized, questions were asked about the woman who had, in effect, saved the boy's life. No one came forward who could identify her. Days later, a photograph was found at the patient's bedside which pictured the boy's mother who had died years earlier. The doctor was astonished when he realized the person who had alerted staff to the medical emergency was the boy's dead mother.

After the training center closed, a team of security guards was employed to patrol the place all night insuring that vagrants and vandals did not enter the grounds. Several guards have reported seeing people, at a distance, wandering the grounds at night yet, on closer inspection no one could be found. The figure most often sited was that of a woman walking near the center's cottages.

Several people who were fortunate enough to get into Fairview after its closure have experienced screams, sobs, voices crying out for help, and even growls. Some fascinating EVP have been captured here that may be accessed online.

This place may be one of the most haunted locations in America but access is severely limited. Surveillance from a position outside the perimeter fence is possible, however.

Infrared imaging, video or still, may capture the many spirits that roam this place at night.

A few years after Fairview's closure, a development group known as Fairview Sustainable Fairview Associates purchased 275 acres and several buildings. In 2004, the Pringle Creek Community was developed on 32 acres. So far, I have not discovered any reports of paranormal activity in the buildings that comprise this development. I would not be surprised is something strange occurs that residents simply don't feel inclined to reveal.

Go to Flickr.com and search for "Fairview Training Center." This site contains 281 photographs and a fascinating history. Also, on You Tube, you can view some amazing stories about Fairview's residents who returned to the place many years after their departure.

* * * *

CHAPTER 6

ASYLUM MURDERS

Old Nevada County Hospital
10433 Willow Valley Road
Nevada City, CA 95959

During my trips to the Grass Valley, near Nevada City, to visit relatives interred in the Forest Hill Cemetery, I often stop at the ruins of the old Nevada County Hospital and wonder about the rumors of misery and documented stories of tragedies that occurred here. This place is unbelievably creepy and a fascinating target for ghost hunters, but there are hazards that should be observed. Aside from the structurally unsound building, there is mold on the exterior. Inside, asbestos and leaded paint peeling from the walls create serious health threats that may be reduced by wearing a mask that covers the eyes equipped with appropriate filters.

In 1860, the first building constructed at this location was designed to house ill and injured patients who were previously treated in a building in central Nevada City. At the urging of the town's residents, county authorities appropriated money to construct a building that was later known as the health, education, and welfare building (HEW). The two-story structure had four wards for men, three for women, with no isolation of patients with mental disorders. When it opened, the hospital was probably state-of-the-art for a Gold Rush era facility. It was reported that ventilation and lighting, corridors, rooms, and wards were adequate, but the four toilet facilities were "not satisfactory." Patients were allowed to bath once each week.

The old Nevada County Hospital in Nevada City, CA.

Over the years, additions to the hospital were constructed, eventually reaching 34,000 square feet. The placed was closed in 1975 and then reopened in 1980 to confine low-risk inmates from the county jail. By the 1990s, the place had become dedicated to out-patient mental health treatment. In 2011, the property was sold to a construction company that planned to build residential units on the land.

Many deaths occurred at this hospital from infectious disease, severe injuries from mining accidents, fires that nearly destroyed the town, gunshot and knife wounds, and congenital disorders. In 1884, it was reported that in te preceding three years, 235 patients were admitted to the hospital with a death rate of 15%. Extrapolating that death rate to the 135 years of hospital service, we may conclude that more than 2,000 patients died in this hospital between 1860 and 1975. At least a few of these tragic souls are believed to haunt the crumbling buildings, perhaps waiting for a gifted doctor or new medicine that would save them.

Ghost hunters who gained access to the building have reported unexplained shadows, and feelings of despair and sadness, and a sensation of being drained of energy. Some have reported a menacing presence and a certain sense that the place is filled with "crazy energy."

A recent tragic event has attracted the attention of many ghost hunters, and a few urban explorers. On January 10, 2001, at 11:30 AM, 40-year old Scott Harlan Thorpe entered the Behavioral Health clinic where he had been receiving monthly treatments for paranoia and agoraphobia. Apparently displeased with the care he had received, he entered the first floor reception area with a gun in his jacket pocket. After the usual greeting by temporary receptionist, 19-year old Laura Wilcox, he pulled the gun from his pocket and fired at Laura through the glass panel, killing her instantly. He then turned the gun on 68-year old Pearlie Mae Feldman, who was sitting in the reception area with a client she had escorted to an appointment that day. Pearlie was fatally wounded.

A health technician, Judith Edzards, was shot several times, but recovered from her wounds. Hearing gunshots coming from the first floor that echoed up the staircase, 35-year old Daisy Switzer, jumped from a second floor window to escape the melee, fracturing more than 20 bones including her pelvis, three toes, four right ribs, and three bones in her spine.

Thorpe continued the murderous escapade in a neighboring town, Grass Valley, where he fatally shot Lyons restaurant manager Mike Markle, and wounded the cook, 34-year-old Richard Senuty. It was reported that Thorpe targeted the workers at this restaurant because he believed they had tried to poison him.

Later that day, after a three-hour stand-off, Thorpe was arrested at his home. Found incompetent to stand trial, Thorpe was found to be not guilty by reason of insanity and sentenced to Atascadero State Hospital. Later, he was transferred to Napa State Hospital (see chapter 24) where he is currently confined.

Many paranormal investigators believe that the intense emotional experience of the shooting at the old hospital has left indelible imprints, or residuals, on the property that create perceptions of misery, fear, pain, and sadness in sensitive people even when standing outside the crumbling walls. Adding to that, we may have the spirits of hundreds of hospital patients who died between 1860 and 1975 roaming the grounds. The structures on this property are closed to the public. Any attempt to enter without permission would be trespassing and fool-hearty due to environmental hazards that may not be readily apparent. Exploration of the exterior may fulfill a ghost hunter's desire for a thrilling with something paranormal.

*   *   *   *

CHAPTER 7

GOLDEN STATE ASYLUM

Site of Mass Graves
Old State Insane Asylum
612 East Magnolia Street
Stockton 95202

Legends and myths about the old Stockton State Hospital are easy to find although little is left of the historic insane asylum. Nearly all of the original buildings have been demolished, leaving most of the facility's one hundred acres as open ground. Today, a few former clinic and support buildings, together with some new additions, comprise the pledging campus of California State University-Stanislaus. Stately Victorian mansions that were once occupied by the hospital's superintendent and doctors still stand on East Acacia Street as a reminder of the hospital facility's great size and the power of its staff over the lives of thousands of patients. To some people, the almost-Gothic appearance of these buildings, and other bizarre remnants, give credence to legends and myths, including ghost stories. When visitors walk the grounds, the sad history of the place is inescapable.

Established in 1853 as the Insane Asylum of California, the facility grew larger each decade eventually housing more than three thousand patients in wards and dormitories. Renamed the Stockton State Hospital in 1896, the facility was closed in 1996. After closure, some of the older buildings stood vacant for a few years and served as venues for local ghost hunters and thrill seekers. Some of the latter have published Internet tales of "dead spots" on the grounds, places where a foul stench evokes vomiting, and locked doors that lead to underground tunnels. These tales might be dismissed as urban myths, but in 2005 several unmarked graves were uncovered on the old hospital grounds that led to investigations by serious ghost hunters and designation of the grounds as a haunted site.

Since 2005, so many unmarked graves have been discovered on the old hospital grounds that researchers have raised questions about how many people remain buried at the site. Between 1854 and 1875, at the site of the women's facility, 510 E. Magnolia Street, 4,467 known burials were done. In 1876, 1,619 bodies were removed to another cemetery nearby on North California Street. More exhumations and reburials were done between 1925-25, but the exact number is unclear. In any case, it seems clear that the bodies of thousands of people who suffered from mental illness remain at the location. Graves of those who died at the facility were not marked with headstones. Wooden markers that indicated graveyard boundaries were burned away in the 1950s by grass fires.

In May of 2007, another forgotten hospital cemetery was discovered at the end of East Acacia Street when workers broke ground for a detention pond. Initial reports indicated thirty graves were found but the true number is almost certainly much higher. When I visited the site in December of 2007, the area was protected by a chain-link fence. The sight of my camera attracted the attention of a security guard who informed me that photography was forbidden without permission of the grounds supervisor. I found this odd since I stood on public ground that comprised the campus of a state university. After speaking to a representative of the grounds supervisor, I was given permission to take photos but informed that I could not publish them. I could not help but wonder if plans for further searches for unmarked graves had created a delicate atmosphere.

There are reports that students have heard disembodied voices, sobs, moans, and screams in some of the classroom buildings that were once used for treatments or dormitories for patients. Disembodied footsteps have also been heard. Chairs have been seen moving across the floor without explanation. At the end of Acacia Street and the former site of the women's facility on East Magnolia Street, sensitive ghost hunters pick up the intense misery, fear, anxiety, and desperation that musty have been experienced by thousands of patient incarcerated here. Paranormal investigators who are skilled with dowsing rods may locate hot spots indicating unmarked graves. Considering the long period of operation of the insane asylum, it would be astonishing if no residual energy remained at several locations on the old hospital grounds.

*   *   *   *

CHAPTER 8

SILICON VALLEY ASYLUM

Old Agnew Mental Hospital
Current: Sun Microsystems Campus
4150 Network Lane
Santa Clara 95054
Press contact: 408-884-4980

For most of the twentieth century, residents of the East Bay Area thought of Napa and Santa Clara as strange places distinguished by insane asylums. In fact, when I was a kid, some of my teachers admonished rowdy students to shape-up or they would be sent to Napa. No one thought of grapes, vineyards, or wineries but the notion of being sent to the Napa, where crazy people were kept, was scary.

As a teenager, when I traveled south from Alameda to San Jose and Santa Cruz for surfing, signs along the highway pointed to the Agnews State Hospital and the idea of being close to insane people made me avoid stopping in Santa Clara.

Today, Napa is a world-class destination for wine lovers while Santa Clara is an integral part of the Silicon Valley, and the home of Sun Microsystems and other high tech companies. Both are attractive communities and desirable places to work and live, yet Napa's State Hospital continues to house more than a thousand patients while some of the Agnews buildings still stand, repurposed for the high-tech industry yet reminding many of the insane asylum.

Opened in 1885, the Agnews State Hospital housed mentally ill patients from around the state, many of them for life. While many patients were docile, some criminally insane persons were also incarcerated there.

It is unknown how many environment imprints were created by the hospital's patients during their lengthy stay. In 1998, Sun Microsystems purchased the 90-acre site and spent $10 million restoring the grounds and four historically significant building but many people still think of the place as a former asylum.

Occasionally, stories are leaked by employees who see or hear bizarre things, but virtually all of these reports are anonymous. Paranormal experiences have occurred in newer buildings that sit on the former sites of patient dormitories or treatment rooms. Apparitions of people dressed in hospital gowns appear for seconds, foul odors are detected, sounds are heard that include screams, sobbing, moaning, bizarre laughter, and unintelligible shouts.

Occasionally, cabinet doors fly open and contents fall to the floor. Investigation by ghost hunters is not possible due to the company's security policies and limited entry to most buildings on the campus, but visitors walking the grounds have had similar experiences.

The expansive campus includes a central treatment building capped by a clock tower that stands eight stories above the ground. In 1889, this building was the primary treatment center where patients were subjected to ice water baths, electric shock, and surgeries such as prefrontal lobotomy. It is likely that hundreds of patients died in this building during these unimaginably stressful procedures. The 1906 earthquake added another 119 patients to the death toll. This un-reinforced concrete structure suffered major damage when walls collapsed onto patients and some staff members. Frequent paranormal activity is experienced by people working in this building but only a few reports have been publicized.

In 2004, three telephone technicians worked inside the clocker tower building installing new phone lines and switching equipment inside a closet. While they worked, strange noises were heard coming from an adjacent small room. After several minutes of hearing knocks on the door, tapping on the walls, and whistling, one of the phone techs opened the door and found the transparent apparition of a young girl standing with her arms out-stretched. When the tech fell back onto the other workers, all three regained their composure and peaked into the small room. The sight of the apparition shocked all three who immediately ran from the building.

The clock tower of old Agnews State Hospital.

I've obtained reports of paranormal experiences from others who have entered the building to perform various renovations that included plumbing, furniture installation, and electrical work. In many instances, paranormal activity is limited to unexplained movement or disappearance of tools, but some workers have reported seeing apparitions of people dressed in gray gowns.

Ghost hunters may walk the campus searching for environmental imprints created by the thousands of patients who suffered years of incarceration at this site. Entry to the clock tower building may be obtained by permission of the security staff.

Nearby, the nineteenth century auditorium, executive mansion, and administration building stand as monuments to the old Agnews asylum.

After touring the old Agnew asylum campus, take a short drive to the site of the old cemetery at 1250 Hope Drive. Located less than half a mile from the asylum's haunted clock tower, the cemetery is surrounded by residential housing. A chain link fence prevents entry, but inside the small museum, a viewing platform allows visitors to view the site where an unknown number of patients are buried.

There are no grave markers and no accessible records that allow an estimate of the number of bodies buried there. However, it is unlikely that many of the patients who died at Agnews before 1900 were claimed by relatives and buried elsewhere. In the nineteenth century, mentally ill people were most often ostracized by their families, sent away to institutions, and forgotten. From 1885 until the 1960s, when more humane treatment was afforded patients, it has been estimated that more than 5,000 deceased patients were cremated and the ashes buried in the Agnew Cemetery.

*   *   *   *

CHAPTER 9

MY HAUNTED OFFICE

Rancho Los Amigos Hospital
7601 E Imperial Hwy
Downey, CA 90242
562-385-7111

The first day I moved into my office in Building 70, on Erickson Avenue, at Rancho Los Amigos Hospital, I knew there was something very weird, and menacing about the place. I had just complete two years of Navy-sponsored medical research at a laboratory on Catalina Island and accepted a position as assistant professor of physiology and physical medicine at a county hospital administered by the University of Southern California Medical School. Given the stature of USC, I expected modern facilities at Rancho Los Amigos Hospital, but I was stunned when I saw the room intended to be my office, and the creepy building that looked as though it had been abandoned decades earlier.

The south campus of Rancho, as we called it, was a large campus of several 2-story buildings covered with pale yellow stucco. One of these buildings – Building 68 - had been renovated into offices for faculty and staff, lecture halls, and a lab. Building 70, location of my assigned office, was still equipped as wards for patients. However, the beds had no mattresses, curtains hanging between beds were dingy and stained, tray tables were covered with greasy dust, and yellow paint on the walls and ceilings was peeling, leaving large patches of a musty paint chips on the soiled floors. Medical equipment had been removed, of course, but IV stands, gurneys, and a few broken wheelchairs were scattered about the two floors. My office on the second floor was clean but dark, with a single dirty window that let in dim light even on sunny southern California days.

As the only occupant of this building, I assumed it would be quiet, allowing me to prepare my lectures. Building 70 was never quiet, however. Often I would heard a soft knock on my door only open it to find that no one there. The sound of squeaking wheels of gurneys and wheelchairs often penetrated the uneasy quiet, especially in the evening when I returned to my office after my 6:00 o'clock lecture in Building 68.

In the morning, when I entered the building, I often encountered the foul stench of urine. Looking around the deserted wards on the first floor, I found no evidence of a recent intrusion by vandals or a homeless person. I noticed that the curtains hangings between the beds would sometimes be expanded, fully enclosing a bed and then, at the end of the day, the same curtains would be pulled back as if patients in adjacent beds wished to visit with each other.

Dark shadows often appeared on the first floor, near the base of the stairs that opened into an area once used for visitation. That creepy feeling of an unseen being hovering over the shoulder was almost a daily experience for me.

The creepiest place was Building 71 which housed the cadaver lab on the second floor. The lab contained 24 bodies that were used in a year-long anatomy class. Two to four students were assigned a body and spent one year dissecting every muscle, joint, nerve, and organ, including the brain. The foul stench of formaldehyde, huge trays of fat dissected from the bodies, and bucket under the tables that collected fluid draining from the cadavers created a nauseating atmosphere that frequently drove many students outside for fresh air. At times, I entered this lab in the evening and encountered a deep sense of sadness. Although I had a compassionate attitude toward the deceased that lay before me, I was aware that this sense of sadness was not my emotion. There was something, or someone in that lab that was deeply saddened by the site of all of those bodies, cut open, picked apart, and destined for cremation at the end of the year.

Old buildings at Rancho Los Amigos Hospital. My office was on the second of the building on the left.

During my time at Rancho Los Amigos Hospital, I was not a paranormal investigator. I hadn't given much thought to ghosts, but I did not deny the possibility that the ghost of a dead person could haunt a place. Within weeks of moving into my office, I assumed the unexplained odors, sounds, shadows, movement of objects, and many other strange experiences were probably ghosts. They didn't frighten or disturb me, so I continued my work without much thought of the history of Rancho and the many spirits that might be trapped there.

Six years after leaving Rancho, I returned to the USC campus to give a lecture for physical therapy students working on a master's degree. After the lecture, I ventured into Building 70 and opened the door to my former office. The desk and chair I had used were still there, covered with greasy dust. As I opened the door, a disembodied voice said, "It's you!" Stunned by the loud exclamation, I stood in the doorway as an icy breeze passed over me, leaving me shaken with the notion that a ghost may have been my office mate during the years I believed I was the lone living occupant of Building 70. About this time, I started studying the paranormal and launched my career as a paranormal investigator.

Rancho Los Amigos Hospital was established in 1888 as the Los Angeles County Poor Farm. Indigents, chronically handicapped, homeless, insane and elderly persons were transferred to Rancho from the LA County Hospital. A campus of 124 acres was opened that contained housing on additional to shops and farm in which residents worked for their room-and-board, or gained skills that enabled them to return to independence. By 1903, over-crowding and poor sanitation prompted extensive renovation that included construction of larger residence halls, or wards.

As the patient population grew, residents were groups according to disability or diagnosis and the poor farm became recognized as a hospital. Mental patients were sequestered in a portion of the campus that was known as Hollydale Mental Hospital or the Downey Insane Asylum. By 1910, Rancho's patient population reached nearly 500 as the campus expanded to 333 acres.

In 1918, the region suffered a Spanish flu influenza epidemic that added to Rancho's patient population and a substantial increase in the campus death rate. It is rumored that many victims of this epidemic were buried in unmarked graves on Consuelo Street near Dahlia Avenue.

During World War II, a portion of Rancho was renamed Camp Morrow and used as a U.S. Army emergency hospital and rehabilitation center for soldiers. After WWII, Rancho's population doubled due to the polio out-break, prompting the construction of several buildings for housing long-term patients including the large, two-story buildings on Erickson Avenue designated Buildings 68 to 72. In many of these building, polio patients were enclosed in iron lungs that sustained breathing until nerves to the breathing muscles would recover. In the

1950s, Rancho gained national preeminence for its treatment of polio victims.

Dark and dismal interior of the abandoned hospital.

By 1956 Ranch Los Amigos Hospital expanded into a north campus and became one of the largest comprehensive medical rehabilitation centers in the U.S. providing services to a wide range of individuals with catastrophic illnesses and injuries. The south campus that was once a poor farm, mental asylum, and hospital - for victims of Spanish flu, the Long Beach earthquake of 1933 that killed 120 and injured thousands, the great LA River flood of 1938, WWII soldiers, and polio - was closed in 1988.

Is Rancho haunted by hundreds of spirits of people who suffered mental illness, severe chronic disability from accidents, disease, and war? Several reports are posted on the internet of paranormal experiences that include the sounds of a baby crying, and faces that appear in the dirty windows, looking outward. Looking inside the building through windows or openings in the sheets of plywood that cover many doors and windows, ghost hunters have spotted humanoid shadows and even a few full bodied apparitions.

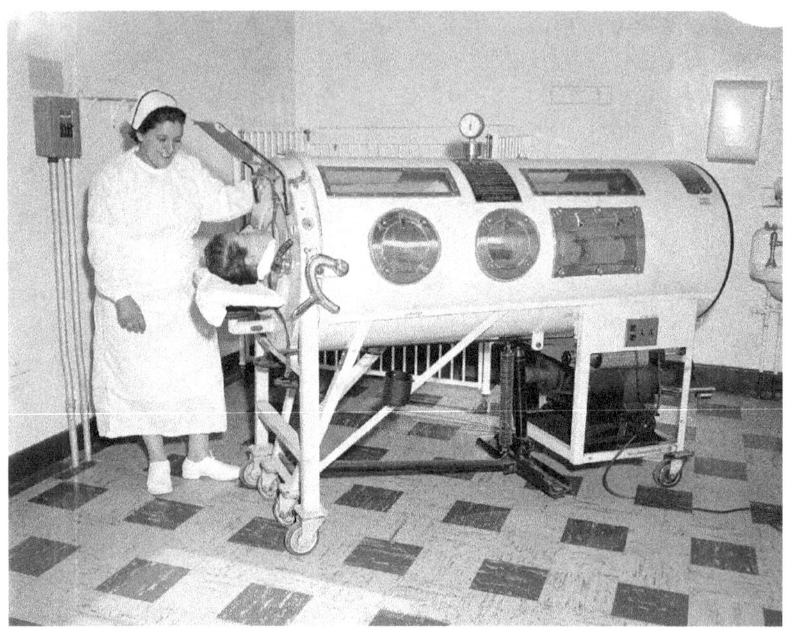

Polio victim being treated with months of confinement in an iron lung.

Is the old Rancho campus haunted? How could it not be The shadow of a short, elderly man, believed to have committed suicide by hanging, has also been reported. Sensitive people, such as myself, who stand at the board-up doorways, have perceived a bizarre force that seems to pull them closer to the door as if a spirit wants company in the dark and dismal old hospital.

* * * *

CHAPTER 10

THE FIRST FEMINIST ASYLUM

Rockhaven Sanitarium
2713 Honolulu Avenue
Glendale, CA 91020
Friends of Rockhaven: 81-248-1707

Years ahead of her time, psychiatric nurse Agnes Richards established Rockhaven in 1923 as a private mental health facility strictly for women who suffered from "mild mental and nervous disorders." Nurse Agnes understood that the rapidly fading idea of a Kirkbride style asylum institution, even on a small scale, was inappropriate for the delicate sensibilities of the women she wished to serve who were "unsettled" by the rapidly expanding Los Angeles metropolis and movie industry. The Cottage Plan was, in her mind, the best solution for treating women with mental "ailments."

"Welcome to a place of rest and rehabilitation for women suffering from overwork and exhaustion." — Agnes Richards. Founder of Rockhaven Sanitarium.

The Cottage Plan gained popularity at the end of the nineteenth century as an alternative to the massive structure dictated by the Kirkbride Model of mental institutions. Following the espoused treatment philosophy of the nineteenth century, the Cottage Plane considered patients to be "residents" or "clients" and treated as guests rather than people afflicted with mental illness. As the name implies, the institution consisted of several cottages, usually one-story and housing no more than two residents. Patios and courtyards provided a serene atmosphere and private place to meet with doctors and counselors rather than a cold, institutional treatment room typical of most mental health facilities in the US at this time.

The grounds of Rockhaven were richly landscaped with shady trees and foliage surrounding tennis courts, a swimming pool, and a golf putting green. The Cottage Plan focused on socialization and development of amicable and firm relationships with staff who were to guide the resident back to the reality of a normal mental perspective and function.

Cottage Plan campuses typically resembled modest resorts with communal buildings encircling the resident's cottage to provide privacy and insulation from the surrounding community. Some of these early Cottage Plan intuitions, such as the Norwich State Hospital in Preston, CT, placed the most violent patients alone in cottages close to the administration building.

As an insulated, private, and peaceful oasis, Rockhaven served many famous people including Gladys Peak Baker (1902-1984) mother of Marilyn Monroe (1926-1962), Broadway actress Billie Burke (1884-1970) who play wicked witch Glinda in the Wizard of Oz, legendary Ziefeld Follies performer Peggy Fear (1903-1994) who died at Rockhaven, and Josephine Dillon (1884-1971), famed acting teacher and first wife of Clark Gable, who died at Rockhaven, and Gwen Lee (1904-1961), a stage and film actress and flapper in silent films of the 1920s.

Ghost hunters may be inspired by the lives of these women and their struggle with mental illness, and entice their spirits to manifest by speaking about their days at Rockhaven, even if they died elsewhere.

During the nine years I lived in Los Angeles, I walked past the walls and gates of Rockhaven several times during visits to friends who lived in the neighborhood. The Spanish Colonial Revival architecture and landscaped grounds always intrigued me, but friends offered cautious advice not to enter the grounds.

Founder of Rockhaven, Agnes Richards, RN. Left, graduation from nursing school in 1922. Right, upon her retirement in 1966.

People looking for ghosts at this historic asylum should reset their approach. Rockhaven was not a place of patient abuse, torture, and misery that was typical of other mental institution in the early twentieth century. Residents were never viewed as insane, though many of them were schizophrenics and paranoid personalities. Ghosts that may be found here are not aggressive or angry. Spirits at Rockhaven appear to be calm and recognize that they are in a safe place, and cared for by compassionate, understanding people. Psychics who have visited Rockhaven told me the place has a serene energy that is strong, but peaceful. Spirits who died here seem to recognize that Rockhaven was a place of salvation, peace, and redemption.

Staff who conduct tours have said that many deaths occurred at Rockhaven, but I have not been able to gain access to records that might tell us how many died here and under what circumstances.

Visitors and staff have reported humanoid shadows in virtually every part of the 3.5 acres campus. A common experience tis to hear doors slamming shut and tapping on windows. Objects once owned by residents of Rockhaven - framed pictures, snapshots, rosaries, notebooks, etc. - are often found by staff during regular cleaning of the rooms, closets, and cabinets that were not present previously. While cleaning a medicine cabinet, a man found a small cache of pills, apparently stashed there by a resident to feigned taking her medicine and then hide the pills from her nurse. When the pills were discovered, the man felt an intense cold cell standing behind him and perceived emotions, including anger and embarrassment, probably generated by a ghost whose deception had been discovered.

During the first three months that a caretaker lived on the premises, he set his clock to the correct time every morning only to find later in the day that it was reset to a random time. After three months, the ghost obsessed with the clock probably became accustomed to the new resident of the cottage, and decided to leave. Rockhaven staff have heard unseen beings speaking in the voice of co-workers, as if mimicking the voices of staff members.

A woman who spend a few weeks at Rockhaven visiting her daughter who worked as a live-in caretaker, reported seeing the apparition of a woman wearing a long white gown, walking the gardens. During a second encounter with this ghost, the spirit looked directly at the astonished woman, beckoning her to come closer.

Agnes Richards retired in 1967 and passed the ownership of Rockhaven to her grand-daughter, Patricia Travis. The placed closed 2006 and quickly became threatened by developers who relished the choice property. The place was saved from demolition in 2008 by the City of Glendale when it purchased it for $8.25 million with the intent of opening the property as a community park.

In February 2016, the site was being considered by the City of Glendale for "adaptive reuse."

An organization called Friends of Rockhaven often stage tours of the famed asylum. For information, call 818-248-1707, or visit www.fridnsofrockhaven.org.

*   *   *   *

CHAPTER 11

REMAINS OF THE DAY

Topeka Insane Asylum
2700 West 6th Street
Topeka, Kansas 66606

The arched driveway that comes off Third Street, now blocked at each end, the circular driveway enclosing what was once a fountain or location of a flagstaff, and pathways that lead to broad open fields now dedicated to recreation, seem to be remnants of some giant estate or institution rather than part of a modern community space called Hummer Sports Park. Looking further, moving into a thick grove of old trees near SW Kanza Drive, ghost hunters and urban adventurers will discovered a stately old building with windows boarded. Offering no entry, it exudes a curious history. A short distance away, also on SW Kanza Drive, sits another brick building of more recent architectural style, labeled with the letter K that also beckons ghost hunters.

Portions of foundations and other remnants of the massive Kirkbride style asylum that once stood here have been cleared from the park, but sensitive ghost hunters find this place eerie at times. A woman who frequents the park with her eight year old autistic child told me her son gets agitated and frightened if the family's recreational activity takes him to the north side of the park, on SW Kanza Street near the intersection with NW MacVicar Avenue, and he gazes across the street at the old hospital's cemetery.

Topeka Insane Asylum was opened in 1872 and dedicated to the treatment of the mentally insane as well as criminals who were deemed unfit to stand trial. At its height, the 80 to 100-acre campus was composed of a massive "bat-wing" style asylum flanking a five-story administration building that resembled a Victorian mansion. The asylum, several shops and other outbuildings were linked by an elaborate array of paved paths that conveyed patients, staff, and visitors through a park-like campus.

Despite the idyllic setting, horrible stories of patient abuse and murder of a therapist led to closure of the asylum in 1997. History suggests the place was managed well until about 1900 when admission standards were relaxed and many were admitted to the asylum without mental illness but with strong tendencies for anti-social behavior. Early in the twentieth century, reports of staff mistreating patients, excessive use of restraints that kept patients in bed for several days, and other inhumane acts began to surface. There are even reports of sexual abuse and rape. A 1913 law that permitted forced sterilization enabled doctors to perform the procedure on 54 patients in 1921. Records are not available for other years.

The practice was continued for more than thirty years before new laws led to its decline and eventual end as a treatment option for mentally ill patients. It is likely that many patients who underwent this procedure are buried in the hospital's cemetery. There has been speculation that their spirits are still in agony from the inhumane surgery.

Events at this asylum became so notorious that by 1988 the hospital lost its accreditation for Federal Medicare and Medicaid payments. The tragic murder of 31 – year old therapist Stephanie Uhlig on February 2, 1992, appears to be the final offense that prompted transfer of patients to other facilities and closure of Topeka State Asylum in 1997.

On February 2, 1992, Stephanie Uhlig and another therapist took 51-year old Kenneth Waddell and a few other patients to a local theater for watch a movie. Upon returning to the hospital, Waddell was the last to be escorted to his room. For unknown reasons, Stephanie was attacked, dragged to a secluded bathroom, and murdered by strangulation. Waddell, 51, was sentenced to three to 10 years for sexual battery and to life in prison for first-degree murder. The space in which this tragic event occurred no longer exists, but the negative energy it generated adds to the eerie perceptions of sensitives who visit this place.

The asylum's cemetery in located on SW Kanza Street about 100 yards west of NW MacVicar Avenue. Covering nearly three acres, it is estimated that 1,157 graves remain at the site. A granite monolith engraved with "Topeka State Hospital Cemetery 1879-1954" marks the grounds where only a few headstones remain. Most of the patient rest in unmarked graves, but in 2006 local mental health advocates raised funds to erect a monument containing the names of all patients buried here.

*	*	*	*

CHAPTER 12

MID-WEST GHOSTS

Ashmore Estate
22645 East County Road North
Ashmore, IL 61912
www.ashmoreestate.net

Ashmore Estates, sitting in a desolate location west of the tiny town of Ashmore and east of Charleston, is an intriguing remnant of the county's former poor farm that also served as a psychic hospital. Well known to viewers of TV shows such as *Ghost Adventures, Ghost Hunters*, and *Ghost Adventures: Aftershocks*, the place has a fascinating history and considerable allure since it was renovated in 2006 as a paranormal venue for inquisitive souls who wanted an up-close-and-personal encounter with a ghost. In addition, documentary films by Christopher and Adrian Booth – *Spooked* (2006) and *Children of the Grave* (2007) – were filmed in the spooky old building. For YouTube viewers, several videos have been posted that present investigations, history, and interviews with ghost hunters who had amazing encounters with the spirits that haunt the place.

The "haunted house" style paranormal venue closed in 2013 due to severe storm damage and then changed hands. In 2014, new owners began extensive renovations and, in 2016, reopened the estate to ghost hunters. Tours, investigations, and over-night stays are now available for investigators who want an asylum experience.

The first structure on the property was erected in the 1870s as an almshouse, or poor farm. Standing two stories tall with more than 4,000 square feet of living space, the place was home to the poor and destitute of the county. It was in this structure that five-year old Elva Skinner died on February 15, 1880. It is certain that several unfortunate people died at this almshouse between its opening in 1870 and closure in 1959. In 1879, superintendent Joshua Ricketts officially reported 32 deaths in the first nine years of operation. Death reports for other decades are not readily available. Many who died while living a life of abject poverty are buried in unmarked graves in two cemeteries.

In 1916, the present structure known as Ashmore Estates was constructed, providing the indigent with modern plumbing, a boiler and heating system, and other amenities. Use as an almshouse ended in 1959 when the building was sold to a corporation that converted the place to a private psychiatric hospital. After only five years of operation, the hospital was no longer private as patients from other mental health facilities were accepted. Over the ensuing twenty years, the business focus of Ashmore Estates changed as additions were made to the 1916-vintage structure. By 1986, however, financial losses were beyond recovery and the place closed.

In 2006, after standing abandoned for twenty years, the place opened as a "haunted house" attraction, building on the suspicion that the creepy place must be full of ghosts. Storm damage and business challenges prompted ownership changes that ended in 2014 when Robbin and Norma Terry opened the place to avid ghost hunters inspired by stories of two ghosts created by documented deaths, and the widespread belief that the short-lived psychiatric hospital spawned several deaths that most certainly created a community of spirits still residing in Ashmore Estates.

Despite dying in 1880 inside a structure that was demolished in 1916, little Elva Skinner is often reported to be an active ghost, roaming the halls of the current structure. History says that Elva awoke one cold morning seeking warmth and moved, unsupervised by an adult, too close to the fireplace. Her nightgown caught fire and she died a heinous death. More than a century later, her ghost haunts a building that replaced her home.

Historical photo of the Ashmore Estate.

Several ghost hunters have recorded EVPs of a little girl's voice pleading for help from the living. EVP also contain Elva's voice asking for her mother. No one has spotted Elva's apparition, but empaths feel the presence of a female spirit, very young, that recognizes she has been badly injured and desperately needs her mother.

The other ghost that gives Ashmore Estates a certain degree of provenance as a haunted location is that of Joe Bloxom (1851?-1921). The exact date of Joe's birth is uncertain. Some sources suggest he was born in 1845 while others indicate his mother, Mariah Bloxom, gave birth in 1852. The details of Joe's final hours on earth are documented in his obituary published in the Oakland Messenger Newspaper (Oakland, Illinois) on June 2, 1921.

The fascinating Ashmore Estates is preserved for ghost hunters in a state of arrested decay.

Known as "Slow Joe," he had been living at Ashmore Estates for fifteen years prior to his death. Late in May of 1921, Joe left the estate to visit friends in nearby Oakland. On Tuesday, May 31, he was in Charleston awaiting a train which would return him to Ashmore. Wandering close to the tracks, Joe was apparently side-wiped by a passing train and sustained significant trauma to his shoulders and back. Feeble and probably in shock, he was found walking toward Ashmore when a passing driver picked home up and delivered him to the estate. Superintendent Harvey Reigel summoned a doctor and moved Joe into the building, possibly the basement boiler room. In shock and likely suffering internal injuries, Joe died at 8:30 PM on Tuesday, May 31. Two days later he was buried in the estate's south cemetery.

Given this history, the frequent and intense paranormal activity in the boiler is widely attributed to Joe Bloxom. Visitors to this space report that creepy feeling that some unseen being is hovering close by. Many have been touched, scratched, or felt a tug on their hair. Isolated spots of thickened atmosphere and cold spots have been reported as well. Ghost hunters report their electronic equipment malfunctions and batteries drain quickly. Sensitive people hear growls emanating from the darkened corners of the room.

In 2015, famed ghost hunter Nick Groff, formerly of the popular TV show Ghost Adventures, investigated Ashmore Estates. While investigating the third floor, Nick's cameraman spotted a black mass move from the hallway into a room. Nick pursed the black mass into the room and captured an eerie EVP that said, "Get out, God dammit!" When Nick asked, "Is somebody following me around in here?" An EVP said, "Yes, I will follow you." In other EVP, the disembodied voice said, Nick," suggesting that the ghost recognized the man who was trying to communicate. Also on the third floor, Nick and his group entered a bedroom and captured an EVP stating, "This is my room."

This investigation, and investigations staged by others, may be viewed on YouTube. Check out "Ashmore Estates Nick Groff Tour" and "Haunting History: Ashmore Estates S04-E05."

Aside from Joe Bloxom and Elva Skinner, other spirits are believed to haunt this place. EVP of an old woman's voice have been captured and sensitives report feeling that rooms on the second and third floors are crowded with spirits, possibly from the twenty-six year period when Ashmore functioned as a psychiatric hospital. It may be useful to note that in the first nine years the place operated as an almshouse, 32 official deaths were reported. If we project that death rate for the entire 89 years of operation as a poor farm, we might concluded that about 288 people may have died on the estate.

Residents of the almshouse who died between 1870 and 1959, and whose bodies were unclaimed by relatives, were buried in two cemeteries. The earliest cemetery is reportedly located a short distance north of the estate. I could not obtain the exact location from anyone I interviewed. The second cemetery is easier to find because the body of Joe Bloxom lies there under a headstone. It is south of State Highway 16 and east of North County Road 2250E. I was given the following GPS coordinates by a resident of Ashmore: latitude 39.5221474, longitude -88.050612. Several headstones have been cleared of debris and 67 internees identified. View the list of persons buried here at:

https://www.findagrave.com/cemetery/2307939/coles-county-poor-farm-cemetery

and then click on "67 added."

Ashmore Estates offers day and night investigations on weekends and over-night public and private investigations.

Contact: https://www.ashmoreestates.net/our-investigations-tours

* * * *

CHAPTER 13

THE DOCTOR'S GHOST STORY

Illinois Asylum for the Incurable Insane
4500 Enterprise Dr.
Bartonville, IL 61607
Phone: (309) 241-3113

A ninety minute drive from Chicago or St. Louis will put you in Bartonville, a small town adjacent to Peoria, on the former campus of the Illinois Asylum for the Incurable Insane. Only twelve buildings remain of the once expansive facility that, in 1927, housed 2,650 patients in 33 wards and clinics with thirty support buildings. Despite the seemingly meager remnants, this place is a popular destination for ghost hunters because of a ghost story published in 1919 by the hospital's highly-respected medical superintendent, Dr. George Zeller (1858-1938).

A fascinating cemetery also beckons fearless paranormal investigators who search for the ghost of A. Book, made famous by Dr. Zeller's intriguing story.

Established by the Illinois general Assembly in 1895, the hospital had an ignominious beginning. A huge structure modeled after the Kirkbride Philosophy for American asylums was completed in 1897 but never used due to structural failure of its foundation. Apparently, its architects failed to notice that it was built over abandoned coal mines that were progressively collapsing. After its demolition, Dr. George Zeller stepped in and directed the construction of a Cottage Plan asylum that consisted of several wards, or dormitories, and clinics, classrooms, shops, and supporting facilities. An impressive three-story administration building of 190 rooms, Bowen Hall, was constructed on land between Constitution Drive and West Pfeiffer Road, west of Industry Road. Opened in 1897, the beautifully creepy building housed some of the hospital's female patients who were incarcerated with their children. For a few years after the hospital closed, the Bowen building was open to ghost hunters, but it was demolished in 2017.

Under Dr. Zeller's leadership, the campus expanded rapidly and included housing for staff, a store, a power plant, and several shops where patients learned skills that might facilitate their return to society. Reflecting his benevolent philosophy regarding the treatment of the insane, in 1906 Zeller opened a nursing school and, a year later, changed the name of the facility to Illinois General Hospital for the Insane. He is also credited with innovating treatments such as light-deprivation rooms and enter-tainment for patients that included a circus, a zoo, picnics, and community outings. Zeller also removed the word "incurable" from the hospital's title to reduce the stigma of mental illness and thwart the pessimistic attitude that insane persons could never be cured, or at least returned to a productive, independent life.

By its twenty-fifth anniversary in 1927, the hospital had served more than 13,000 patients and developed a reputation quite different from asylums that started operation in the nineteenth century. A strong vocal advocate for benevolent treatment of the insane. Dr. Zeller invited reporters, government officials, and other doctors to tour the hospital. He famously rid the place of restraint devices and refused to use isolation and various forms of punishment as a means of controlling unruly patients.

A major shift in hospital policies occurred when Dr. Zeller retired in 1913 and his replacement, Ralph T. Hinton MD ordered bars placed on all windows and use of restraint devices such as cages and straight jackets. Hinton also closed the zoo, stopped outdoor entertainment and other activities Zeller had introduced as a methodology for enculturating patients to society. Deterioration of the hospital forced Hinton to relinquish his position to Dr. Ralph Goodner.

The Bowen building at Peoria State Hospital, Illinois.

During Goodner's three years as superintendent, the hospital suffered a plague epidemic that killed 150 patients and a rapid deterioration in care. Dr. Zeller returned as superintendent in 1920, but decline of the hospital was set in motion and he was unable to reverse it.

In the early 1930s, a syphilis outbreak affected many patients, and staff, and patients started hanging themselves in the woods surrounding the hospital. Zeller retired in 1935 and moved to an apartment in Bowen Hall when he died in 1938. From that date to the hospital's closure, misery became the best descriptor of Zeller's ideal mental asylum. In 1967, a nurse was killed by a patient. In 1972, patient Bernard Roe was struck in the head with a chain as he stood in line waiting lunch. He died several hours later. Patient Jerome Spence was beaten to death by an inmate with a 3 year old mentality.

Dr. George Zeller (1858-1938).

At its peak in the 1950s, Bartonville housed 2,800 patients. As community-based mental health services developed in the US, the census of large asylums steadily declined. By 1972, the patient population at Peoria State Hospital was less than six hundred. In that year, the hospital was closed and a thirty-year process of demolition of its buildings began. Today, only twelve buildings remain, repurposed to private businesses including the popular Peoria State Hospital Museum ((309- 232- 8794). When many of the hospital's buildings were demolished, bulldozers pushed tons of debris, including plates, cups, bed frames, hospital equipment, personal belongings of the patients, and clothing into nearby ravines. To this day, some of these remnants surface after winter rains and cause local ghost hunters to speculate that the massive collection of asylum remnants holds spirits on the property.

Aside from ground-breaking, benevolent treatment of patients developed by Dr. Zeller, this asylum is best known for the story of a patient known as Old Book and his ghost. In his 1935 memoir, *Befriending the Bereft,* Dr. Zeller immortalized this unfortunate patient with a detailed report of the man's ghost.

"Old Book" was a nickname given to a mute man who was admitted to the hospital around 1910 at the age of 22. Unable to speak, the staff derived a name for the man who was believed to be employed in the printing business as a book binder. "Bookbinder" seemed appropriate, so he was named A. Bookbinder (1878-1910). Later, someone referred to him as Manuel, possibly because he was assigned work as a manual laborer, primarily digging graves. It is unclear as to why he was referred to as "Old Book," because he was only 32 years old when he died of tuberculosis.

It is said that, after each grave he dug, Old Book stood by the burial and wept for the deceased. His out-pouring of emotion during the frequent burials ingratiated him to the hospital's staff and he came a favored patient. When Old Book died, his burial was officiated by Dr. Zeller and attended by more than 200 staff. It is said that when his coffin was raised over the open grave, it felt unusually light, causing the men to stumble to the ground. The stunned crowd quickly speculated that Old Book's body might not be within the casket, so it was opened. When the body was found within the casket, the ghost of Old Book appeared at a nearby elm tree, sobbing uncontrollably. In his book, Dr. Zeller mentioned that hundreds of people saw the ghost and verified that it was Old Book. Apparently, over the ensuing years the ghost of Old Book appeared at several funerals, standing at the elm tree, weeping for the deceased.

Some years later, Dr. Zeller ordered the elm tree cut down, but work was stopped when the men assigned to the job reported that the tree screamed each time it was struck by the axe. The fire department was called to burn the tree, but the flames were extinguished when the fire captain reported visions of a man standing in the flames, screaming. Eventually, the rotted tree fell and its remains were hauled away.

This fascinating but seemingly implausible story has been discounted by some as a fanciful tale designed only to commemorate a beloved patient. Reportedly, Dr. Zeller wrote that the story was a fabrication intended to preserve the memory of a patient loved by himself and the staff. A disclaimer, of sorts, was included in *Befriending the Bereft*. Others have pointed out that none of the hundreds of witnesses of Old Book's ghost wrote about it. I suggest that the disclaimer included in Zeller's book, that the ghost story was a fiction, was added only to thwart critics who might criticize Zeller as a feeble-minded old doctor who had spent too much time with the insane. As for the apparent lack of reports by others who witnessed Old Book's ghost, with the possible exception of some of the doctors, the staff would have included only a few who were inclined to write an article for a newspaper or magazine in 1910. A description of an encounter with the ghost of an asylum patient would have ended the career of nurses and doctors.

Many ghost hunters who visit the hospital's grave yard search for the ghost of Old Book. EVP sweeps that include questions about the process of digging graves or Dr. Zeller's compassionate care of Old Book may capture some amazing audio phenomena created by the ghost of a man who was mute throughout the latter years of his life.

The old hospital's museum houses an amazing collection of relics from the days of Dr. Zeller to the asylum's ultimate decline and closure. Aside from photographs and maps, the place houses some creepy devices such as the cage that confined patient Rhoda Derry (1834-1904) for decades until she was transferred to Peoria State Hospital under the care of Dr. Zeller, blind, insane, and emaciated from food deprivation. The museum is located at 4400 Industry Road.

Patients who died at Peoria State Hospital, and whose remains were unclaimed by family members, were buried in four cemeteries. Rhoda Derry (1834-1906), a long-term patient who suffered many decades in a cage, is buried in grave 217 in

Cemetery One on South Becker Road near the Lord's Table Church of God church.

Cage used to restrain patient Rhoda Derry for decades

Cemetery Two is south of the hospital campus on Enterprise Road. Manuel A. Bookbinder is in grave number 713. Cemeteries three and four are north of cemetery two, behind a building that was once the Pollak TB hospital at 4500 Enterprise Drive.

This structure now houses a paranormal venue called the Haunted Infirmary:
(http://www.hauntedinfirmary.org/).

* * * *

CHAPTER 14

ASYLUM OF SEVEN STEEPLES

Former Indiana Hospital for the Insane
Central State Hospital
3045 West Vermont Street
Indianapolis, IN 46222
Museum: 317-635-7329

In 1827, the Indiana state legislature became one of the first in the nation to establish a state-wide mental health policy, but construction of a hospital was delayed until 1848 when a small building, serving only five patients, was placed on one hundred acres of land outside the city limits of Indianapolis. Citizens of the city tolerated the small insane asylum only because it sat a considerable distance from the town's central district, west of the White River. Additional buildings were constructed between 1850 and 1889 as the patient population grew to more than one thousand.

In 1889, the name of this facility was changed to Central Indiana Hospital for the Insane as additional mental hospitals were constructed in other parts of the state. By 1926, with a patient population of 3,000, the name was changed once again to Central State Hospital. Covering hundreds of acres, the asylum consisted of two ornate buildings - one for men and one for women - constructed according to the Kirkbride Plan. The women's hospital became known as "Seven Steeples" because of its unique architectural elements. Additional buildings included a large power plant, administration building pathology laboratories, clinics for occupational therapy and acute illnesses, a chapel, recreation hall, auditorium, bowling alleys, a bakery a fire house and a cannery staffed by patients. Patients also worked in the gardens, orchards, and farms, and tended the grounds.

In 1950 patient population reached 2,500 despite demolition of the men's asylum in 1941. By 1970, many structures dating from the nineteenth century had been demolished and replaced by mid-century institutional architecture typical of government buildings. Central State Hospital continued to serve patients until 1994 when charges of patient abuse became widely known and inadequate financial support forced its closure.

Today, only a few buildings remain on the expansive campus including the pathology lab (dating from 1895) that is now a museum, the administration building (1936), power plant (1886), carpentry shop (1937), men's recreation hall (1939), and laundry (1894). A remnant of particular interest to ghost hunters is the maze of tunnels under the campus. Reportedly, five miles of tunnels were constructed as conduit for pipes and electrical cables, and to facilitate movement of staff and patients between buildings during periods of inclement weather. These tunnels are rumored to have contained dungeons in which unruly patients were chained to walls and tortured.

Like many major mental institutions of the nineteenth century, Central State Hospital (CSH) was founded on the benevolent precepts of the Kirkbride Plan and the treatment philosophies espoused by Nurse Dorothea Dix. By 1870, however, Superintendent Dr. Orpheus Everts (1826-1903) became appalled at the treatment of patients at CSH and abuses perpetrated by staff. In a report to the governor, he stated, "basement dungeons (are) dark, humid and foul, unfit for life of any kind, filled with maniacs who raved and howled like tortured beasts, for want of light, and air, and food, and ordinary human associations and habiliments..." He described wards without adequate light, heat, and ventilation, and iron frames covered with straw used as beds for patients. Dr. Everts also demanded repair of the hospital's rotten floors, insect infested pantries, and leaking ceilings, and campaigned to rectify many violation of the hospital's philosophy of "moral treatment."

In 1883, in a great bonfire, Everts' successor directed staff to burn the hospital's straight jackets and restraints, and other devices he considered inhumane.

Despite these altruistic campaigns, CSH has a long legacy of misery that was widely publicized. In 1886, the Dallas Morning News reported a CSH patient was beaten by a male attendant in bathroom and another was kicked and rendered unconscious by slamming his head into the floor. In 1896, 35 year old Samuel Strauss committed suicide by hanging himself with his suspenders from a transom in the men's recreation hall. In 1919, the Fort Wayne News Sentinel reported patient Thomas Edwards used an iron bar discarded by repairmen in the laundry and bludgeoned to death an attendant and 75-year old Mary Kelly.

There are several unsubstantiated reports of patient abuse in the tunnels that led to death. A widely circulated story centered on the tunnels featured a low-risk patient named Alvin who was permitted to walk the grounds without supervision. One day, Alvin failed to return to his ward and extensive search was launched that failed to find him. Assuming he had left the hospital, the matter was closed with the expectation he would return someday.

Years later, a young woman named Agnes admitted to a nurse that she sat daily by a tunnel entrance conversing with a man named Alvin. Suspecting Alvin was somehow living in one of the tunnels, a searched was conducted that discovered his body.

The official record of this event, of course, did not conclude that Agnes had been visiting with Alvin's ghost, but it seems likely. Ghost hunters who have gained access to the tunnels look for Alvin. Some fascinating EVP have been captured in the tunnels with a male voice that says, "Where. . ." and "Need light."

The old power plant on the campus of the Central State Hospital in Indianapolis, IN., slowly decays.

In the old power plant basement, ghost hunters have captured EVP of a screaming. There are rumors that patients were cremated in the furnace which offers a tantalizing notion that the ashes shoveled by night workers into waste bins contained the remains of many patients. At many locations within this building, humanoid shadows have been spotted at times when the boilers, when in use, were turned on and off.

In the carpentry shop, many ghost hunters, including me, have heard whispered conversations immediately upon entering the building as if living persons have interrupted a social gathering of ghosts. Some of these ghosts have even questioned the intruding by asking, in an unearthly voice, "What are you doing here?"

The old pathology building was converted to a museum in 1990 and by 1994 became the depository for more than 15,000 items pertinent to the medical history of Indiana. This place is fascinating, but super creepy. It contains an autopsy room, refrigerators in which dead bodies were kept, medical instruments, tissue samples, a lecture hall, and many other artifacts that will inspire every ghost hunter.

The grounds of this former asylum contain at least four areas that contain the bodies of patients who died and remained unclaimed by family or friends. Grounds at the corner of Tibbs Avenue and Vermont Street, known as Section 1, received the first burials between 1848 and 1905. Three additional burial grounds – designated Sections 2, 3, and 4 – are located on the west side of Tibbs Avenue near Washington Street, close to the Mount Jackson Cemetery. Currently, 575 graves have been discovered, some marked only with a stone or identified by ground-penetrating radar.

In 2014, archeologists from Ball State University used ground-penetrating radar to locate bodies of patients interred in unmarked graves. This multi-year process was hampered recently by recent projects on the property that involved digging trenches for a new water line intended to serve the police department's new K9 training facility. Working without an on-site archeologists and observance of applicable laws and regulations intended to protect historic sites, crews unearthed the remains of three persons and crushed the bones. After archaeologists were alerted and arrived on the scene, they were able to exhume ten additional bodies whose final resting place was in the path of the water line.

These disturbing events often arouse spirits. They've also aroused the interest of local ghost hunters who target Section 1 for some exciting paranormal experiences. Bizarre lights have been spotted hovering over the burial ground that include streaks of blue light flashing across the area about three feet above the ground, and flashes of light described a "miniature ball lighting."

Another place that fascinates ghost hunters is the Indiana Medical History Museum (www.imhm.org). Located in the old pathology building at 3270 Kirkbride Way, this place contains some truly creepy stuff including medical instruments, skeletons, old textbooks on insanity, an operating room, medicines, and slices of brain tissue revealing tumors. It even has a replica of a 1950s doctor's office with furniture, instruments, and other artifacts from the office of Dr. Marion Scheetz of Lewisville, Indiana.

The Indiana Medical History Museum is housed in the former pathology labs of Central State Insane Asylum.

Is this place haunted? IMHM staff denied having experienced any paranormal activity, but some visitors have posted comments online about creepy sounds emanating from the basement when no one is known to be in that space. The creep factor intensifies when visitors learn that this building was used to perform autopsies on patients who died at Central State.

Like many old asylums that once covered more than a hundred acres somewhat removed from a city's business district and finer neighborhoods, Indianapolis eventually grew and surrounded the asylum's property making the land valuable for modern development. In 2003, the city purchased 160 acres of asylum land for $400,000 and renovated several buildings for use as administrative centers, archives, and a state library.

Over the ensuing years, developers purchased additional remaining structures, or demolished others for the construction of apartments. A valuable map published in Wikipedia indicates newer construction, buildings that remain from the nineteenth century asylum, the former location of the "seven steeples" women's wards, and the surgical wards.

Section 1 cemetery is located in the northwest portion of the campus adjacent to the intersection of Tibbs Avenue and Vermont Street.

*   *   *   *

CHAPTER 15

THE LITTLE GIRL'S ASYLUM

The Beard Building
Wayne County General Hospital
30712 Michigan Avenue
Westland, MI 48186

Not much remains of the once expansive Eloise Psychiatric Hospital, but remnants of the place remain on the radar of many ghost hunters because of a creepy cemetery, the haunted Beard building, inspiration gleamed from a popular movie called *Eloise* (released in 2014), several intriguing videos posted on You Tube, and a strange name, borrowed from Eloise Dickerson Davock (1888-1982), the daughter of Detroit's first postmaster.

Eloise's father was Freeman Dickerson, who served many years as Wayne Country's superintendent of the poor. In 1894, Dickerson used Eloise's photograph for fund raising events. Apparently, the little girl's likeness attracted so much attention, while garnering substantial financial gifts, that locals began referring the hospital as Eloise's place, or simply Eloise. In 1911, the sprawling facilities were officially named Eloise Psychiatric Hospital, the Eloise Infirmary (Poorhouse), and the Eloise Sanatorium for treatment of tuberculosis patients. In 1945, the place was renamed Wayne County General Hospital and Infirmary. In 1979 it was officially called Wayne County General Hospital, with the psychiatric division closing in 1982.

Like many asylums, Eloise started as a poorhouse in 1839 with 35 residents who, despite their mental impairments, worked as laborers in the dairy barns, pig farm, root cellar, tobacco curing warehouse, and greenhouses. Over the next one hundred years the place grew, reaching a peak population of 10,000 during the 1930s. At one time Eloise was the largest psychiatric facility in the US, consisting of 78 buildings with a staff of more than 2,000. In 1958, as hospital admissions declined, farming operations ceased, and some of the land was sold to developers. Most of the mental health wards were standing vacant in 1973 and by 1977 official plans for closure were implemented. The last psychiatric patient left Eloise in 1982. Four years later, the general hospital closed.

Today, only 5 buildings remain standing. D building, eponymously designated the Kay Beard building, stands facing Michigan Avenue. It housed as many as 400 patients in wards and included living quarters for many employees, including the Catholic chaplain. After closure, the 150,000 square-foot building was used for county offices. It was vacated in 2016 when plans for conversion to a senior living facility were developed. In recent years, the vacant building has been the venue for a popular paranormal tour.

The firehouse, which also served as a laundry, and the power plant are decayed and probably unsafe to enter. The bakery was set ablaze by arsonists in 2016. Its ruins will likely we hauled away in the near future. The former commissary – now the Samaritas Center – serves the community as a family homeless shelter.

For many years, Eloise was known as a cutting-edge hospital. During the tuberculosis epidemic that started in 1903, doctors instituted novel treatments that included separation of patients ("social distancing") and fresh air exposure and use of X-rays for diagnosis. Eloise continued to operate the free-standing TB hospital until 1923. In the 1950s, Eloise doctors treated psychiatric patients with hydrotherapy, sensory deprivation chairs, and twirling chairs. Some treatments, deemed essential and successful by doctors but now viewed as abusive, included insulin therapy, straitjackets, shackles, and lobotomies.

Eloise enjoyed a good reputation until the Depression Era (1930-1939) when over-crowding and poorly trained staff inevitably led to abuse of patients. It was reported that as many as 3,800 mental patients, including many with TB, were housed in quarters designed for 2,500. In 1934, 50% of the hospital's population suffered from mental illness while most of the remaining patients were destitute, uneducated, and plagued with chronic illness. Demands on the staff were over-whelming and reduced the attention and care that each patient received. Consequently, boredom and atrophy were rampant.

Visitors reported that many patients sat in chairs or on the floor all day, staring at walls or outward through dirty windows without discourse with other patients or staff. Reports began circulating in local newspapers of staff who beat patients, employees who stole supplies and food, mismanagement of hospital funds, and unsanitary conditions. One reporter found that only five toilets were available for use by 125 women. Abuse also included widespread use of electro-shock therapy and lobotomy for management of unruly patients. Over the course of 150 years, it is certain that many thousands of patients died at Eloise. The cemetery on Henry Ruff Road contains the remains of more than 7,000 patients. I could not locate records that detailed the number of deaths in each year of operation, but it is likely that far more than 25,000 died here.

Most of the visitors who tour the decayed Bear building experience something paranormal. In a video entitled, *Scary encounter from Eloise Psychiatric Hospital,* recorded on the third floor of the Bear building, Todd Bonner of Detroit Paranormal Expeditions (DPX), heard footsteps, doors and drawers opening and closing. The audio recording indicated these sounds were nearly continuous over five minutes. Members of this group also posted spirit box recordings that clearly demonstrate a ghost claiming that it created nausea and dizziness in living persons, and directing a person reclining on a bed to "sit up." Others, standing outside the Beard building, have reported foul odors, sounds resembling a hammer hitting metal pipes, and partial apparitions that appear humanoid. The apparition of a woman wearing a white gown or hospital robe, has been spotted in the upper floor corridor and on the roof.

Empaths who enter the second and third floors have reported debilitating emotions that range from depression and total despair to intense anger and rage. One of my associates from Chicago felt such intense, energy-draining emotions that she had to be carried from the building.

It is common for ghost hunters and those participating in the history tour to hear disembodied voices on every floor and encounter isolated cold spots. Some have reported growling, sobbing, laughter, screams, coughs, and conversation between unseen beings. Visitors who snap photographs routinely find unexplained light anomalies in captured images, including illumination from ceiling lights in a building without electrical service. On rare occasions, ghosts have reportedly thrown objects at visitors and spread broken glass on the floor. Unexplained puddles of water have appeared in several rooms on the third floor.

The first Eloise cemetery was located northwest of the facility, but those bodies were moved in the late 1890s to an island in the reservoir that was eventually filled in to create Michigan Avenue. It is unclear if those bodies were moved, once again, when the avenue was paved in 1910. Another cemetery was opened south of Michigan Avenue and east of Henry Ruff Road. It has been reported that in the late nineteenth century, medical students from the University of Michigan snatched bodies from this cemetery for dissection.

A third cemetery that attracts ghost hunters is located further south on Ruff Road. Used for burials from 1910 to 1948, this cemetery contains the remains of more than seven thousand patients, including many children. Essentially a "Potter's Field," this cemetery was used to bury those whose body was unclaimed by relatives. With a few exceptions, graves are marked only with a concrete block engraved with a number.

Much of the paranormal activity at this cemetery has been attributed to patients who suffered incurable mental or physical ailments, died young, and were buried in an unmarked grave. My local colleague, Greg Sanderson, has captured video of light anomalies hovering over many of the graves. He has also recorded EVP of sobbing, screaming, and cries for help that include, "Find me," and "When am I?"

Ghost hunters who plan to visit Eloise should first view notable postings on YouTube that include *Sneak Peek Inside Eloise Asylum, Exploring the Eloise Psychiatric Hospital (Parts 1 and 2),* and *Scary encounter from Eloise Psychiatric Hospital.* Ghost hunters might also be interested in a history lecture: *The History of the Wayne County Poorhouse and Asylum – Eloise.* This asylum also inspired the horror movie *Eloise,* released on February 3, 2017, by Vertical Entertainment. The Travel Channel's television show *Destination Fear* filmed at the location for the seventh episode of their first season.

Tours of Eloise's Beard building and grounds are offered by Eloisehauntedtours@gmail.com. Phone: 313-355-0721.

*   *   *   *

CHAPTER 16

SEGREGATED ASYLUM

The Jemison Center
6th Street off of 5th Street
Northport, AL 35476
GPS coordinates: 33.227654, -87.629672

This unbelievably creepy hospital should not be confused with the Old Bryce Hospital, located in nearby Tuscaloosa that opened in 1861 under the name Alabama Hospital for the Insane. Considered an exceptional example of Kirkbride Plan architecture for mental health facilities, that expansive hospital was renamed for its first superintendent, Peter Bryce, who was considered a pioneer of humane psychiatric care. With a patient population that once numbered 5,000, the huge structure operated until 2010 when it was sold to the University of Alabama. An $80 million renovation plan preserved the main building and its cupola and created facilities for the department of theater and dance. The new Bryce Hospital opened in July 2014 at 1615 Ruby Tyler Parkway, in Tuscaloosa, and currently serves about 250 patents.

The abandoned asylum, often mistakenly referred to an Old Bryce Hospital, was actually called the Jemison Center and established in 1933 to treat mentally retarded and handicapped boys. The land was originally part of the 4,000-acre Cherokee Tract plantation originally owned William Jemison. In 1932, a portion of the old plantation was sold by Jemison's descendants to the state of Alabama for construction of a satellite facility to relieve over-crowding at the Bryce Hospital. This facility was the State Farm Colony for Negroes, opened in the era of Jim Crow laws and policies. William Jemison's plantation home was demolished and in its place a three-story structure was erected, with the traditional southern-style columns gracing the main entrance, and three out-buildings housing a heating plant and shops.

It is rumored that the Jemison Center's inmates, segregated from mainstream mental health care at Bryce Hospital because of their race, were selected from other facilitates because they were able to work in the fields of the old plantation without pay. These mentally impaired but able-bodied patients produced their own food, manufactured furniture, and worked at other tasks under the guise of "therapy."

When the Jemison Center ceased operations in 1977, some of its patients were transferred to the nearby S. D. Allen Intermediate Care Facility which closed in 2003. Under the harsh southern climate, the old Jemison building quickly deteriorated. With the collapse of the roof, every window was broken, painted peeled from the walls, foliage grew throughout the interior, and soil and animal droppings accumulated on the floors. Even before its closure, this place was in deplorable condition.

In 1970, a reporter from the Tuscaloosa News reported: "Human feces were caked on the toilets and walls; urine-soaked aging floors; many beds lacked linens; patients were sleeping on the floor. One small shower served 131 male patients; the 75 female patients only had one shower. Most of the patients at Jemison were highly tranquilized and appeared to have not bathed in days. All appeared to lack any semblance of treatment. The stench was almost unbearable."

Under such horrible conditions, it isn't any wonder that patients with mental illness probably suffered worsening of their physical and mental health. I was unable to locate records of patient deaths, but it seems certain that in its forty-four years of operation, many patients died here, alone, unbathed, malnourished, and afraid. There is no record of a cemetery for patients on the property, but it seems likely that many of the deceased, unclaimed by relatives, were buried in unmarked graves. The Jemison family cemetery, sitting north of a warehouse at 1441 Industrial parkway, contains the remains of Confederate Senator Robert Jemison (1802-1871), Priscilla Cherokee Taylor Jemison (1812-1886), wife of Robert Jemison, William Jemison (1778-1829), Sarah Mims Jemison (1784-1826), wife of William Jemison, and Minerva D. Betts (1838-1886).

The Jemison Center is now is such an unstable condition that entry is unsafe. Visitors who stand outside the building report sensations of "bad energy," spine-rattling chills, and a huge cloud of misery that hangs over the decaying structure. A few brave explorer and paranormal investigators have entered the building and experienced some of the negative energy created by the misery of those who languished in filthy beds and suffered from the racist attitude of those who were charged with delivering humane care. Several images of the interior may be viewed online at:

https://abandonedsoutheast.com/2019/08/25/jemison-center/.

Ghost hunters have reported hearing footsteps, screams, sobbing, and muted coughs. Cold spots have been detected even in the heat of summer. Several inches of accumulated filth on the floors, strange inscriptions on the walls, and several heavily soiled mattresses contribute to the disturbing impression of ghostly anguish. A red substance on the walls that appears to be paint has been claimed by some visitors to be blood from animal sacrifices. Empaths feel intense oppression, typically generated by the misery of living persons, but sustained by spirits of the dead.

Currently, entry is unwise because the building is structurally unsound. Added to that, the debris and filth that fills the hallways is most assuredly a health hazard. Ghost hunters have experienced the intense imprints of fear, loneliness, despair, pain, physical illness, and mental aberrations simply by standing next to the exterior walls of this place. Some have reported unexplained lights inside the center and even humanoid shadows.

*   *   *   *

CHAPTER 17

GHOST OF THE FLAPPER GIRL

Ghost of the Flapper Girl - Zelda Fitzgerald
Former Highland Hospital
19 to 75 Zillicola Street
Asheville, NC 28801

In 1904, Dr. Robert S. Carroll established an insane asylum in downtown Asheville. Proving unpopular with the business community, he moved the asylum to Zillicola Street in 1909. Known originally as Dr. Carroll's Sanatorium, this colloquialism probably reduced the anxiety of others living in the upscale neighborhood until 1912 when the name was changed to Highland Hospital for the Insane. The hospital was composed of a campus that included a number of mansions, three of which still stand. Many ghost hunters, and some residents of this beautiful neighborhood, believe these remaining buildings, and open land on which patient wards once stood, retain the ghosts of inmates who died in a horrific fire in 1948.

Built in 1895, Rumbough House stands at 49 Zillicola Street. This 9,000 square foot mansion was once the administrative center for the asylum. Nearby, at 75 Zillicola Street is Highland Hall. Built in 1900, this huge mansion was used for patient admission interviews and treatment, and possibly as a discharge center for patients who were returning to their families. A later addition to the sprawling hospital campus was another mansion known as Homewood.

Homewood at Highland Hospital, Asheville, NC.

Constructed in 1927 as a residence for Dr. Robert S. Carroll and his family, the spectacular building at 19 Zillicola Street covers 13,143 square. Its crenelated tower, tall chimneys, flying buttress, and massive stone walls resemble a Medieval European castle far more than part of an American hospital complex. Clearly, Dr. Carroll was fascinated by European architecture which inspired an imposing structure to stand as an extension of his authority. The interior was equally impressive with high ceilings and hardwood floors.

Between Homewood and Rumbough House a 4-story building once stood that included kitchens, meeting and treatment rooms, a morgue, and patient's rooms.

Dr. Carroll was medical director of this asylum until 1939 when he donated the building to Duke University, located in Durham, as he assumed the position of the university's medical director. His patients were generally from wealthy families or those with some celebrity, who suffered from mental illness and nervous diseases, including the famous Zelda Fitzgerald.

Born in Montgomery, Alabama, as Zelda Sayre (1900-1948), her path to celebrity started with her April 3, 1920, marriage to up-and coming author, F. Scott Fitzgerald. History identifies Zelda as one of the first "flapper girls." This moniker distinguished young women who wore short skirts and short hair, listened to jazz, drank in excess, used heavy make-up, smoked cigarettes, drove cars, and engaged in casual sex. Even before she married Scott Fitzgerald, Zelda had a reputation as a wild girl with complete disdain for proper behavior stipulated by polite society. Despite her irreverent behavior, she had many devoted friends who described her as charming, intelligent, shrewd, funny, and pretty. Zelda also suffered from mood swings that stressed her marriage.

In 1924, Scott and Zelda joined other American expatriates in Paris and spent time with iconic personalities of this period including Ernest Hemingway, Alicia B. Toklas, Gertrude Stein, Pablo Picasso, and Salvador Dali. During this time the marriage suffered due to Scott's heavy drinking, Zelda's frustration with her inability to launch a literary career which would match that of her husband's, and the endless parties that led to accusations of infidelity. In April 1930, Zelda moved to France and was admitted to a sanatorium where she was diagnosed as a schizophrenic. Later, she was moved to a clinic in Montreux, Switzerland. She remained a resident of that psychiatric hospital until 1932 when she returned to the US. In the ensuing year, Zelda became violent and reclusive. In 1936, Scott contacted Dr. Carroll and secured Zelda's admission to Highland Hospital in Asheville, North Carolina.

Scott described her state of mind in a letter to friends: "Zelda now claims to be in direct contact with Christ, William the Conqueror, Mary Stuart, Apollo and all the stock paraphernalia of insane-asylum jokes. For what she has really suffered, there is never a sober night that I do not pay a stark tribute of an hour in the darkness. I was her great reality, often the only liaison agent who could make the world tangible to her." Despite that statement, Scott admitted that his alcoholism contributed to Zelda's mental disorder. He last saw Zelda in 1938 before moving to Los Angles where he died in 1940. She remained a resident at Highland Hospital until her death in1948.

Highland Hospital fire of 1948.

Late in the evening of March 10, 1948, Zelda was in her room on the fourth floor of the hospital, likely sedated as preparation for electroshock therapy treatment. Apparently, her nurse locked the door after leaving the room. Moments later, a fire erupted in the kitchen when an electric coffee maker malfunctioned. At 11:35 PM, Nurse Doris Jane Anderson entered the kitchen and discovered a table covered with flames. She described the flames as "one of those fiery hoops animals jump through in circuses." In her testimony, he explained her failure to extinguish the blaze by saying she had never previously encountered a "destroying" fire. Within minutes, the fire rose to the second and third floors of the building by way of the dumb-waiter shaft.

Minutes later, the fourth floor was involved and flames spread across the roof. As hallways filled with smoke, patients and staff made their way to fire escapes only to find the wooden structures engulfed in flames. Most of the doors leading to the internal staircase were locked, as were most of the windows. Without fire alarms and sprinklers, there was no time for staff members to evacuate the upper floor.

While the city's fire brigades raced to the scene, a nearby resident, police Captain Harold Enloe, was the first arrived at the scene. In his testimony, he stated, "I could hear screaming on the third floor. Flames by then were lapping through the roof of the building."

Zelda Fitzgerald, about 1925.

Eleven female patients were rescued, but nine women died by this fire; two died after rescue by fire fighters. Seven victims, including Zelda, were trapped on the fourth floor. Tragically, a week before the fire, Zelda had been discharged with plans to return to her mother's home, but she chose to stay another week at Highland Hospital insure her readiness to leave after a ten-year stay.

Zelda's body was so badly burned that identification was made by dental records and a single slipper that remained on her foot. The dead also included Mrs. Allen T. Hipps, Mrs. W.B. Kennedy, Mrs. Ida Engel, Mrs. Jules Doering, Miss Janice R. Borochoff, Miss Marthina DeFriece, Mrs. V.W. James and Mrs. G.C. Womack.

On the grounds of Highland House, on the northeast side near the driveway, is a plaque that remains as a memorial to Zelda Sayre Fitzgerald. On the plaque is a quote from a letter Zelda wrote to F. Scott. It reads: "I don't need anything except hope, which I can't find by looking backwards or forwards, so I suppose the thing is to shut my eyes."

Although more than seventy years have passed since the great fire, and the Highland Hospital no longer exists, ghosts of those who died on Zillicola Street have been spotted by locals and ghost hunters.

Some have reported sighting the ghost of Zelda who stood 64 inches and weighed, at the time of her death, 130 pounds. Since Zelda was known for taking daily walks around the hospital campus, many assume the ethereal figure seen between Homewood and Rumbough House is Zelda's ghost.

A former hospital employee has reported an encounter with the ghostly Zelda who, he claimed, looked at him with a trouble facial expression as though she were trying to recall his name.

Other spirts have been spotted included a young man who may have died at the hospital years before the fire, and two women, walking arm-in-arm, who may have died in the great fire.

Psychics who have visited Zillicola Street report several spots at which the atmosphere thickens and turns icy cold even on warm evenings. EVP of a muted scream has been captured along with a women sobbing.

*   *   *   *

CHAPTER 18

AMERICA'S LARGEST
LUNATIC ASYLUM

Trans Allegheny Lunatic Asylum
50 South River Avenue
Weston, WV 26452
www.trans-alleghenylunaticasylum.com
304-269-5070

The Trans Allegheny Lunatic Asylum (TALA) stands as the holy grail of paranormal investigation. Now open as a haunted attraction that entices curious tourists and supremely experienced ghost hunters from all over the country, the massive venue, spooky architectural style, an arcane history that includes murder and suicide, and intensity of paranormal activity make the place deserving of the designation as the most haunted asylum in America. In addition to thousands of visitors each year (pre-pandemic), the asylum has been featured on nearly every paranormal TV program including: SyFy's *Ghost Hunters* and *Ghost Hunters Academy;* Travel Channel's *Ghost Adventures, Paranormal Challenge, Portals to Hell, Ghost Stories,* and *Destination Fear;* and Destination America's *Destination Lockdown.* In addition, there are several high-quality videos posted on YouTube and may serve as a *briefing* or orientation for ghost hunters who want to be prepared for what

could be the most thrilling investigation they could ever imagine. The distant location – 130 miles from Pittsburg, PA, and 100 miles from Charleston, WV – does not stand as a barrier to an amazing paranormal adventure available through day and evening tours and over-night investigations offered by the asylum. For information visit;
http://www.trans-alleghenylunaticasylum.com/main/hauntings.html.

For those who are fascinated with the place, but don't want to risk an encounter with a paranormal entity, a history tour is also offered at:
http://www.trans-alleghenylunaticasylum.com/main/heritagetours.html.

Construction of this Kirkbride-style iconic asylum began in 1858 and continued for many years as additional buildings were added to the facility that covered nearly 700 acres. Initial work on the foundation was performed by convict laborers. As work on the massive superstructure progressed, stonemasons were imported from Europe to add structural and decorative elements in Gothic Revival and Tudor Revival architectural styles including a 200-foot-tall clock tower completed in 1871. When the main building was completed it stood as one of the largest hand-cut stone buildings in the world. Today, it is superseded only by the Kremlin in Moscow.

In 1864, the first patients were admitted to wards designed to house 250 people. At its peak, the asylum's patient population exceeded 2,500. Throughout its history TALA was plagued by problems that affected many large asylums including over-crowding, severely limited supervisory staff, poor sanitation, insufficient furniture, poor lighting, and inadequate. Designed to be self-sufficient, the sprawling facility included: vegetable gardens; a dairy herd; a coal mine; gas and water works; barns for pigs, goats, and chickens; horse and carriage barns later used for trucks and cars; and a cemetery.

The iconic Trans Allegheny Lunatic Asylum.

Throughout the later decades of the nineteenth century, shops were added in which patients manufactured clothing, curtains, fabrics, furniture, and mattresses, fulfilling the philosophy widely held by American asylums that the institution should be self-sustaining while teaching patients a trade that might enable them to be independent upon discharge.

Aside from wards for patients, meeting and treatment rooms, surgery suites, and bathing facilities, many of the doctors and staff lived in apartments in the asylum.

Opened in 1864 as the Trans-Allegheny Lunatic Asylum, stigma attached to the words *lunatic* and *asylum* prompted the state of West Virginia to change the name in 1913 to Weston State Hospital. It could be argued that WSH was a more appropriate name for this facility because many people were admitted with behavioral problems arising from a medical condition, and other questionable ailments, that would not be considered mental illness by leading physicians of the era. The list of reasons for admission to TALA from 1864 to 1889 included laziness, masturbation, menopause, excessive religious enthusiasm, belief in superstitions, learning disabilities, mental retardation, marital discord, consumption of bad whiskey, dissipation of nerves, immoral life, jealousy, political excitement, spinal irritation, novel reading, venereal excesses. Many were admitted because of drug abuse, epilepsy, alcoholism, and autism. In 1935, a 4-story, brick tuberculosis building was added which, over its lifetime, housed thousands who suffered and died from TB.

When the place was reopened as a tourist destination in 1994, the original name was reinstated, a museum was established, and some of the patient rooms furnished to represent the asylum as it appeared in the late nineteenth and early twentieth centuries.

Despite the grand architecture of the Kirkbride style asylum and effort to create a state-of-the art institution for treatment of the mentally ill according to the philosophy of Dorothea Dix, TALA declined throughout much of the twentieth century due to over-crowding (at times, 5 to 6 patients were placed in a room designed for one), high turn-over of staff, and other problems such as several fires, one of which severely damaged the fourth floor in 1935. Neglect of patients by unskilled staff, punitive "treatments," isolation of patients from their families, food shortages, extensive use of the antipsychotic drug Thorazine, and poor sanitation became general characteristics of the place. Patients who were designated as "unable to be controlled" were locked in cages called "confinement cribs."

The introduction of experimental lobotomy in 1950 - performed on more than 4,000 patients – resulted in many serious operative complications that included a near-vegetative state, and hundreds of deaths. Many deaths at TALA were suicides or murder committed by patients who were allowed to roam freely throughout the grounds and wards.

On May 18, 1963, Muriel C. Creamer, an African-American housewife from Charles Town, WV, was admitted to a room on Ward. A week later, she was found dead, in her bed, by psychiatric aide Wanda Jacqueline Reed. Muriel was found with restraints at her feet and waist to confine her to bed. Cloth wrapped around her neck, possibly a bed sheet, led investigators to conclude Muriel's death was a homicide by strangulation. The case was never fully resolved, but Muriel's room-mate, patient Wanda Maxine Janes, reportedly admitted that she committed the murder because she believed "improper advances" had been made toward her.

On September 27, 1992, patient David Michael Mason, 29, choked George Edward Bodie, 46, to death in a ward on the third floor. Five years earlier, Mason and his accomplice, James Woods, were charged with first degree in the death of Dean Metheny, 49, and with the malicious wounding of Raymond Diller. Mason was not prosecuted for that crime due to his mental incompetency. It has been reported that he was sufficiently lucid to avoid charges by blaming the death on a ghost in the room.

In October of 1992, the decomposed body of 21-year-old Brian Scott Bee was found by a guard. The official report indicate Brian had been missing for eight days prior to discovery of his corpse.

A cemetery filled with unmarked graves, a history of suicides, murder committed by patients on other patients, and the likelihood of sexual abuse are part of the institution's dark history which now contributes to its celebrity as the most haunted insane asylum in America.

Out of a long, dark history that must have generated thousands of ghosts, a few spirits of TALA patients have become well-known to staff and frequent visitors. Many paranormal investigators who visit TALA have had encounters with the ghost of Lily, a little girl believed to have died in the asylum at the age of 9 years. Few details have been discovered in official records that verify the legend yet is widely believed that Lily was born in TALA or became a resident of the first floor when her mother was admitted as a patient in the 1920s.

An alternate story tells us that Gladys Ravensfield gave birth to Lily in 1863 after she was admitted to the asylum following her rape by several soldiers.

Lily is known as a playful ghost, often grasping the hand of visitors and tugging on shirts, skirts, hand-bags, and back-packs. She sometimes communicates by manipulating flashlights and moving toys (rolls ball) brought by ghost hunters as trigger objects. YouTube videos reportedly show a ball placed in motion by unseen hands when ghost hunters specifically ask Lily to "roll the ball." Lily may contribute to the sounds of children playing which include laughter, running, skipping, and humming.

Despite her playful nature, many sensitives get the impression that Lily is sad because she cannot find her mother. Many believe her mother died at TALA on an upper floor and she is unable to move to the floor where Lily manifests or she is completely unaware of her location. EVP have captured a female child's voice saying, "Mom, where's my mommy?" Lilly manifests most frequently in the Civil War section of the asylum.

Another spirit specifically sought by frequent visitors is Jacob who occupies rooms and corridors of the Civil War section of TALA. Believed to be a soldier admitted in 1864 with emotional disturbance that we might label Post-traumatic Stress Disorder, Jacob manifest by coughing, laughing, and marching around his room as if he is wearing heavy boots. He has been heard whispering threats such as "Gonna get you," that have been captured on audio recorders.

Sensitives who visit his room perceive a foul odor that has been attributed to a foot wound, raising suspicions that he suffered from gangrene of a foot wound. Awareness of his wound, and its foul odor, may explain why Jacob seems to be attracted to women who enter his room wearing alluring perfume.

Perhaps the most intriguing haunted site within TALA is a room once occupied by patient Dean Metheny (1937-1987). In 1987, Dean was placed in a room with David Michael Mason, aged 24, who was known as a violent offender. Some sources claim Dean was mute and, perhaps, that is why he could not call out for help when two patients attacked him, allegedly because of his "annoying behavior." That behavior may have been Dean's apparent refusal to speak with the men. Unaware that Dean was mute, they may have felt insulted when he did not replay to their questions. In any event, the two patients were enraged. They pulled a sheet from the bed and tried to hang Dean from over-head pipes. Failing to kill him, they pushed Dean to the floor and positioned a bed post over his head. Mason then jumped on the bed, driving the bedpost through Metheny's skull. Mason was not prosecuted for that crime due to his mental incompetency. It has been reported, however, that he was sufficiently lucid to claim innocence and blame the death on a ghost in the room.

Dean Metheny's room is a hot spot for ghost hunters. A collection of coloring books remains on Dean's bed because coloring was his favorite activity. People who enter Dean's, a deaf-mute in life, report he 'speaks' through the process of electronic voice phenomenon. He also enjoys communicating through other ghost hunting gadgets, turning flashlights on and off, and giving gentle hugs to visitors

On September 27, 1992, patient David Michael Mason, 29 committed his second murder at TALA when he choked George Edward Bodie, 46, to death in a ward on the third floor. Deemed incompetent to stand trial, Mason remained incarcerated for the remainder of his miserable life.

In a corridor on the second floor, visitors often hear a voice that is readily recognized by former nurses or orderlies who visit TALA or now serve as tour guides. Apparently, an elderly patient known as old Ruth was moved, in her wheelchair, to a location in a corridor on a daily basis to provide visual and social stimulation absent in her small, dark room. Apparently, Ruth was not one to suffer fools or tolerate intrusion on her personal space. Visitors walking the corridor near her former room hear her spirit say, "Go home damn you!"

Grant Wilson and Jason Hawes, founders of the much celebrated The Atlantic Paranormal Society (TAPS), captured evidence of a full bodied apparition they dubbed the "crouching doctor" (Season 4, episode 9). Attracted to the muted sound of coughing that seemed to emanate from an empty room in the Civil War section, these investigators entered the room and spotted a humanoid figure that appeared to be crouching with hands raised above its head. Appearing as a dark shadow, no details could be discerned. Within seconds, the shadow figure moved rapidly across the floor, giving the impression it was sucked out of the room. Following airing of this video segment on the TV show, Ghost Hunters, the room was visited by enthusiastic ghost hunters who reported feeling an unseen hand grab their clothing, back-pack straps, and hair. There is a report on the Internet of one visitor being pulled from the hallway towards the room. It was reported that her companions had to literally sit on her to keep the mysterious force from pulling her across the floor.

Another site that may interest ghost hunters is a room on the third floor, Ward C, not currently mentioned as a haunted location. On May 18, 1963, Muriel Creamer was admitted and confined to her bed with restraints. On May 25, she was found about 9:00 PM by psychiatric aid Wanda Reed who was performing her usual duty of bed checks. It has been reported that Muriel was found with a cloth around her neck, possibly a bed sheet. The death certificate listed the cause of death as homicide by strangulation by a bed sheet.

When questioned, Muriel's room-mate, Wanda Maxine Janes admitted that she strangled Muriel because she had "made improper advances" toward her. No specific mention of Muriel's ghost has been posted on the Internet but Ward C seems like a good target for ghost hunters. This ward was known by staff members as "hazardous duty" because most of the patients were difficult to control.

It has been reported that staff often walked the hall in pairs, "back-to-back," to guard against patients who would try to grab keys that hung from a belt. Ghostly sounds have been reports on this ward that include screams and cries, and women's voices

During tours, visitors may hear the whispered voices of TALA's ghosts call for help, or comment on clothing or hairstyle. Sobbing, moans, crying, and screaming are heard throughout the asylum. Voices speaking in French, Spanish, and German have been reported.

Several apparitions have been spotted, including Lily in a white dress, and a man is a long night shirt. In addition, crawling, crouching, standing and floating shadows have seen in several locations. Foul odors have been encountered that include horses in the Civil War section where animals were stabled during construction, urine, feces, halitosis, and the stances of infected wounds.

Sensitives report the perception of depression, anger, fear, despair, and anxiety, particularly in the drug addiction wards. At times, the perceptions are so strong that people have had to leave the buildings. Tactile sensations are common and include unseen hands touching hands, arms, ears, of visitors. Women with long hair may feel ghosts pulling or stroking their hair. Straps hanging from backpacks and hand-bags are easy targets for ghosts.

Patients who died at TALA succumbed to a vast array of illnesses, accidents, suicide, and murder. Notable suicides that attract the attention of ghost hunters include Peter Morris who hung himself on November 12, 1892 and Gunther Scnell who reportedly died of "strangulation" on August 12, 1891, possibly by a belt, rope, or other device.

On April 16, 1938, Michael Parfeniewtz ingested lye. Many infants who were borne at TALA, and toddlers and very young children who resided there with their mother who had been admitted for mental illness. Literally thousands died of TB and other respiratory diseases, cardiac illnesses, hypertension, diabetes, cerebrovascular disease (strokes), infections.

As many as 20,000 bodies that were unclaimed are buried in the asylum's cemetery. Most have no grave marker, or a concrete block engraved with a number. A few monuments document the life of the person interred six feet under. If you are looking for a specific patient, or relative, consult Sheri

Brake's excellent history of TALA, *Haunted TALA* for a list of names.

* * * *

CHAPTER 19

HOME FOR ABANDONED PEOPLE

Forest Haven Asylum at Fort Meade
Center Avenue at First Street
Fort Meade, Maryland 20755

Opened in 1925 under a banner of altruism, as a true haven dedicated to the most humane treatment of the mentally ill, Forest Haven asylum slowly declined to one of the most abusive mental institutions in America with one of the highest death rates.

Sited on nearly three hundred acres of forested land only twenty miles from Washington DC, the asylum was planned as a state-of-the-art treatment center with open grounds that enabled patients to experience the calming effects of nature. Gardens and a dairy farm provided patients with opportunities to learn skills that might sustain them after discharge. Every effort was made to create an environment that would met the specific needs of individual patients. Wards were established according to the Cottage Plan and given pleasing names such as Magnolia, Pine, Oak, and Hawthorne. In 1938, the asylum was expanded with the construction of the administration building which contained 38 hospital beds, two fracture beds, 18 cribs, an operating room, lab space, an x-ray room, a dentist's office, and a psychiatrist's laboratory. First Lady Eleanor Roosevelt attended the dedication ceremony on March 8, 1940.

During the WWII years, the asylum maintained high standards despite a growing patient population. Two-hundred acres of woods surrounding the campus provide a calming atmosphere, but wards and treatment areas became overcrowded and many staff were placed in positions for which they were not qualified.

By the 1950s Forest Haven faced financial problems resulting in discontinuation of many services and a reduction in staffing. Urine soaked mattresses and mal-nourished patients became common. Admission standards were also changed resulting in a patient population that was untenable. Forest Haven became a dumping ground for patients without mental illness but plagued with chronic conditions such as blindness, seizures, mental retardation, and deafness. In 1974, twenty orphans from a nearby orphanage were relocated to Forest Haven after they were reclassified from "orphan" to "retarded." By the late 1960s, abuse of patients became a frequent occurrence.

Throughout the 1970s and 1980s, families of abused residents filed hundreds of complaints and many lawsuits against Forest Haven. Documentation of horrific cases of patient abuse, including wrongful death, was sent to the Justice Department to enlist legal support and the exceptional investigative capacities of the department. In 1978, recognition by the courts of the irreversible misery of the asylum led to orders to transfer 1,100 residents to other facilities, leaving fewer than 250 in the deteriorating facility. On June 14th, 1978, Judge Pratt ordered the closure of Forest Haven in a statement known as the Pratt Decree. Legal proceedings would delay the final departure of patients until September of 1991. On October 14th, 1991, the asylum officially closed with an official death total of 387 but high suspicion that hundreds more were unaccounted for due to lost or destroyed records. In a brief period between 1989 and 1990, ten deaths were recorded when the patient population was only 252 residents.

Today, the buildings that comprise this asylum are undergoing continuous decay. Most of the windows are broken, allowing snow and rain of winter and hot humid air of summer to enter. In many places, ceilings are collapsed and light fixtures hang from exposed wires. Floors are littered with debris composed of paint that peeled form the walls, broken tiles, glass, and leaves blown through the windows by winter storms. In many rooms, furniture remains, including desks, chairs, file cabinets, sofas, bookcases, gurneys, patient beds, and treatment tables. Equipment remains in the dentistry clinics and surgery suites. Much of this discarded stuff is coated with animal droppings. Many walls are covered with graffiti and red paint intended to give the impression of blood. It is amazing that many files, notes, and other records remain in offices and on the wards. Many of these documents clearly display the names of patients and doctors, medications prescribed, and assessments of mental and physical disorders.

The funding reductions that began in the 1960s led to horrific stories of patient abuse were ultimately well-documented. Medically incompetent doctors and un-qualified nurses, orderlies and therapists contributed to a culture of neglect and abuse aimed especially at patients who were difficult to control. Heavy restraints confined patients to urine-soaked beds or cribs. Excessive use of sedatives, food deprivation, isolation, and sexual abuse became standard operating procedure.

In 1962, 9-year-old John Kennedy, Jr., as admitted to First Haven due to seizures, learning disability, and hyperactivity. Within weeks of his arrival, his mother discovered that all of his teeth had been removed. During a visit, she saw him standing naked against a wall while an orderly showered him with high-pressure water.

Patient Bertha Brown, who suffered from a compulsive eating disorder, was left unattended on a toilet. She died from choking on her own feces. Patient Earline Thornton was given medication to treat pain arising from a fractured hand she suffered in a fight. Family members suspect she was over-dosed when the Earline continued to complain of pain and swelling. Sometime after the last administration of medicine – probably Thorazine – she was found dead in her bed in Match of 1977.

One of the best-documented case of patient abuse concerns 17-year-old Joy Evans. Admitted when she was eight years old, Joy's behavior problems cause staff to tie her to her bed and fed her in the supine position. As a consequence, Joy aspirated food into her lung and developed aspiration pneumonia. Choking was a common reaction to this feeding procedure, but the raging infection that followed proved fatal. Joy died at the age of seventeen in July of 1976.

Despite rampant destruction of the asylum's buildings by vandals and homeless people, few ghost hunters have investigated the place because the grounds are guarded by US Park Police, and formal request for entry are denied because of the hazardous condition of the structures. Fascinating videos posted on YouTube by urban explorers who have entered the asylum may serve as a detailed orientation for paranormal investigators who might gain entry by application to the Federal Park Service.

My interviews of brave and clever adventurers who have spent hours inside the asylum suggest that every floor of every building harbors ghosts and a vast array of paranormal imprints. Humanoid shadows are virtually everywhere as are thick "cells" of air that may be inexplicably cold. Whispered voices are heard as if the speaker were at a distance, down a darkened hallway although on many occasions the unseen speaker sands close behind the ghost hunter. Nearly every ghost hunter who enter the decayed buildings captures EVP on audio recorders or video recorders. Many of these recordings contain the sounds of sobbing, crying, screams, moaning, or men and women begging for "Help." One poignant EVP is that of a woman sobbing followed by "I don't want to die here."

From 1928 to 1982, patients who died at Forest Haven Asylum were transported to the basement morgue where a cursory examination would lead to a declaration of the cause of death. In most cases the cause of death was attributed to common illnesses such as heart failure, stroke, bowel obstructions, influenza, and diabetes. In some instances, patients died of drug over-dose, particularly from Thorazine which is known to cause severe heart rhythm abnormalities that could be fatal. During the last decade the asylum housed patients, many died of aspiration pneumonia caused by forced feeding while the patient remained tied to a bed. In this posture, food and liquid easily entered the trachea of the patient, especially those who resisted the feeding procedure. Bacteria on food particles, together with vomit from the stomach, entered the lungs causing the infection that characterizes pneumonia.

It is estimated that more than five hundred patients were buried in the cemetery, despite as official death total of 387 patients. Many of the bodies were placed in crude wooden coffins transported to the cemetery by dump trucks. A metal disk, placed between four graves, engraved with numbers designated the occupant of each of the graves. A master list of 387 names salvaged from asylum records was used to create a granite monument that stands at the cemetery as a memorial to all those, named and unnamed, who occupy the graves of the Garden of Eternal rest.

The cemetery, located about 2,000 feet north of the asylum's administration building, may be reached by River Road.

*   *   *   *

CHAPTER 20

ISLAND OF MASS GRAVES

Hart Island Asylum
New York Parks and Recreation Department
WWW.NYCGOVPARKS.ORG

Sitting in Long Island Sound, only a few miles from Manhattan, Brooklyn, and Queens, Hart Island is a microcosm or collection of monuments to New York's dark history. On this tiny island, comprised of only 131 acres, more than thirty structures once stood including an insane asylum, hospital for the "feeble-minded" and alcoholics, a quarantine station during the cholera epidemic of 1870, a reformatory for boys and young men convicted of crimes, a prison-of-war camp, a work farm for the indigent, a drug rehabilitation center, and a jail for unruly Union Army soldiers. The Civil War era and Cholera epidemic of 1866 resulted in the earliest burials on Hart Island, but after its purchase by the City of New York in 1868, the place truly started to fill up.

The most recent estimate indicates about one million bodies are buried on the island with interments averaging 1500 each year. With such as monumental number of graves, nearly all unmarked, Hart Island is a hard target on the radar of many paranormal investigators.

Hart Island became a historical entity during the Civil War when it was commandeered from the owner and used as a training facility for the 31st Infantry Regiment of the United States Colored Troops. In addition to barracks that could house up to 3,000 troops, the camp included a commander's house, a library, and a concert room. Advantages of the island's isolation led to construction of a prisoner-of-war camp used during the final four months of the war that incarcerated more than 3,000 Confederate soldiers. Two-hundred and thirty-five of them died in the camp

In 1868, the island was sold to the city of New York as an ideal location for the city's indigent population of sick, mentally ill, incorrigible, dangerous, alcoholic, and drug-abusing persons. Over the course of fifty years, several building were constructed that included not only treatment centers, reformatories, and jails, but also housing and other facilities for staff. Much of the construction was accomplished with labor provide by prisoners from nearby Riker's Island.

Following the Civil War, the small cemetery on the island inspired the notion that Hart Island was an ideal cemetery for the refuse of New York society. By 1870, indigent persons who died in New York's hospitals and on the streets were placed in plywood boxes and shipped to Hart Island. Over the ensuing century, some of the 800,000 boxes shipped to Hart Island contained only body parts gleaned from dissection laboratories at the region's medical schools. Other contained the remains of still-born births and children under the age of five years.

By 1913, burials became an industrial process with huge trenches opened in the earth that could accommodate three boxes stacked vertically and twenty-five across. In some plots as many as 250 "coffins" were interred and marked only with a plot number. After 25-50 years, the buried remains were considered sufficiently decomposed that the trenches were reused after bulldozers crushed the remnants of previous burials. Much of the work of opening trenches, off-loading coffins from the ferry and placing them in the trenches, was performed by prison-labor.

Sometime before 1900, the island became known as New York's "Potter's Field," a colloquialism for a cemetery that contained the remains of poor people or those unclaimed by family. As burial's continued throughout the twentieth century, Hart Island became known as the world's largest tax-funded cemetery with an estimated internment of 850,000 bodies by 1970. The AIDS epidemic of the 1980s added bodies that were buried in trenches separate from others because of fear that the corpses could spread HIV. Later, when it was clear that this could not happen, the city interred AIDS victims in the mass graves.

Historic photo of convict laborers loading coffins
into Hart Island trenches.

During the COVID-19 pandemic in New York City, the city's mortuaries became over-whelmed resulting hundreds of temporary burials for victims. Although in April 2020, New York City mayor Bill de Blasio stated that Hart Island was only being used to bury unclaimed corpses, it was used for deceased who had, in their will's chosen it as a burial place. In 2021, the website *The City* reported a sharp increase in the number of interments between 2019, when 846 corpses were buried on the island, and 2020, when more than 2,000 corpses were placed in the island's infamous unmarked graves.

As excellent video embedded in a Wiki-pedia posting about Hart Island may be viewed at:

ttps://commons.wikimedia.org/w/index.php?title=File%3ACOVID-19_burials_on_Hart_Island.webm.

Some of Hart Island's buildings have been demo-lished to make way for mass burials, but several remain standing that are likely haunted. On the island's eastern shore, the 1910-vintage carriage house was used to store supplies ranging from hardware, cooking equipment, bedding, electrical gear, and food. By 1940, it served as the island's morgue where bodies were held prior to exportation to other cemeteries. South of the Carriage House, also on the eastern shore, the Dynamo House may be found by its tall smoke stack. Built in 1912 of convict labor, it housed the power plant and several shops where inmates learn trades such as shoe-making, laundry, and butchery.

Two hundred feet to the west is the Pavilion. Once of the largest remaining structures on the island, the Pavilion served as lunatic asylum and charity hospital. Further to the west, a Catholic Chapel stands overgrown with vegetation. Built in 1931 at a cost of nearly one million dollars, the chapel served mainly the island's staff. The one and one-half story red brick structure was abandoned in 1966 when the island's workhouse closed. The local arch diocese removed the stained glass windows, leaving the structure exposed to the harsh climate and birds.

Facing the west shore of the island, a square two-story building stand as a remnant of the prison record repository. It has been reported that thousands of pages or records containing personal information of inmates still litter the floors while other records rot inside rustic filing cabinets. Nearby, the reformatory is similarly littered with bedding, clothing, rustic furniture and animal droppings. Built in 1910, the reformatory housed young men convicted of misdemeanors and designed as a rehabilitation center rather than a prison. Owning to the island's isolation, no bars were placed on the windows. Inmates were taught trades such as shoemaking, iron work, landscaping, and cemetery care. Asbestos in this building, and several other on the island, creates a hazard for anyone who gains access.

Near southern tip of the island, and clearly visible to boaters and kayakers, the early-twentieth century hospital stands facing City Island. The hospital focused on chronically ill patients and those with tuberculosis. Short-stay mental illness patients were also housed here along with alcoholics. This huge structure could accommodate 2,000 patients. From 1967 to 1976 the building housed the Phoenix House for drug treatment where some inmates were sentence by a judge to five years of treatment.

Other places on Hart Island that may be an anchor point for ghosts or imprints, or comprise a vortex, include an obelisk that marks the burial site of twenty Union soldiers who died before 1865. Other sites include the peace monument built in 1948 by inmates, The Mercury School Ship memorial, which contains the graves of two boys who drowned in 1878 while training on the ship, and 600 grandstand seats removed from Ebbet's Field in Brooklyn in 1960.

It comes as no surprise that Hart Island has not been investigated by the casts of popular paranormal TV shows or local groups of ghost hunters. Access has been severely limited to a viewing area known as the gazebo. However, many inmates from Riker's Island prison and contracted workers have spent several days on the island. Was able to contact some of these men and inquired about their experiences on the island loading hundreds of coffins in to trenches. Naturally, all of them demanded anonymity because of their criminal history.

Based on these brief interviews, Hart Island is possibly the most haunted place on the planet. Men who have worked on the island have had many repetitive paranormal experiences. Working near the Pavilion, Reformatory, Power House, and many of the trenches filled before 1930, a massive volume of whispered voices often arises from the still air and fills the minds of workers. Embedded in this barrage of sound are voices of children asking for asking for help. At times, the request is clear.

Where is my mother? Why am I here? Help me! I am lost! Did I die! I don't want to be here. It hurts, please help me! Don't let them hurt me!

On overcast days and late afternoons under winter skies, workers have seen unexplained lights in the hospital, power house, and administration building. Loud "popping sounds have also been heard echoing through some of the structures. "Weird, creepy feelings," were reported by two of the men I interviewed who opened some of the older mass graves to install new residents.

The men who buried the dead on Hart Island are often imprinted with the process, coming away from the place, and release from prison, with an indelible imprint of misery, pain, sadness, fear, and hopelessness. Take a look at:

Hart Island - The Saddest, Most Haunted Place in New York and https://i95rock.com/hart-island-the-saddest-and-most-haunted-place-in-new-york/?utm_source=tsmclip&utm_medium=referral.

When Hart Island opens to wide-ranging visitation policy in the latter part of 2021 we will hear some amazing reports that will convert even the most stalwart skeptic.

The process of visiting the island has been improved due to efforts by the Hart Island Project and the New York Civil Liberties Union. In July 2021, access is expected to open when jurisdiction over the island is transferred from the Department of Corrections New York's Parks and Recreation Department.

The Hart Island Project helps individuals with family members buried on the Island track down loved ones and negotiate visits. The organization's mission is to assist families and individuals to gain access to public burial records and information concerning burial procedures on Hart Island, and increase public awareness of the history of Hart Island, and the Potter's Field in New York City, through "engaged storytelling." Contact at www.hartisland.net.

* * * *

CHAPTER 21

VILLAGE OF THE DAMNED

Letchworth Village
Letchworth Village Road at Ridge Road
Thiells, New York 10984

Like so many mental institutions founded in the early twentieth century, Letchworth Village, in picturesque Rockland County, New York, opened in 1911 with the best intentions and greatest aspirations for improving the lives of people afflicted with mental illness. Named for American business man and philanthropist, William P. Letchworth (1823-1910), the village might more properly be considered a city that ultimately consisted of more than 130 buildings spread over two thousand acres. The initial plan, recognized by contemporary progressives as a departure from the almshouses and massive asylums of the nineteenth century, included architecture inspired by Thomas Jefferson's Monticello with separate dormitories and training rooms for children and adults, and spacious parks for outdoor recreation.

The 1927 *Rockland County Red Book* noted that facilities were, "sub-divided as far as possible in order to avoid the tendency toward institutionalism." Many of the patients received instruction in skills that might someday sustain them after discharge by working several farms and producing enough food to support the entire population of the village. Some loaded coal into furnace rooms or were put to work constructing nearby county roads.

A sign that the asylum was slipping off the tracks might be found in Dr. Charles S. Little's 1921 report in which he divided the village's population into three categories: those who were "feeble-minded," a "moron" group, and an "idiot" group. The latter, he suggested, should not be housed at Letchworth because they could not work or be otherwise productive in a way that would benefit the state.

Despite the support of charitable institutions and the state of New York, by the early 1920s the place had a reputation for patient neglect and abuse, unqualified staff, and mismanagement. Internal reports leaked to newspapers described patients wandering the halls in soiled and torn clothing, showing signs of malnutrition, physical illness, and lack of bathing. Rumors circulated of patient abuse by staff members that included with-holding food as a means of punishment, and restraint in chairs for long hours.

Staff members were also guilty of abusing co-workers that included sexual harassment and rape. Reports of food shortages and unclean water were made but denied by administrators. Still, visitors to the institution noted filthy corridors and bathrooms, discarded rash, and dirty windows.

Much of the rapid decline of Letchworth was due to over-crowding. In 1921 the patient population was 1,200. By 1935 it was 3,500. Fifteen years later it swelled to more than 4,000 with as many as seventy patients in a dormitory room designed for thirty. Among patients admitted by medical practitioners were hundreds of others that were abandoned at the steps of the administration building by their families. Letchworth reached its peak patient population of 5,000 in the late 1960s.

The beginning of the end for Letchworth may have occurred in the late 1940s when photographer Irving Haberman released several photographs for public view that documented the terrible conditions of the asylum. Dirty, half-naked patients huddled in cramped dayrooms revealed by these photographs started a series of investigations that continued until the village's closure in 1996.

The few buildings remaining at Letchworth Village are filled with debris that may make visits hazardous.

A hallmark in the lengthy investigative period was Heraldo Rivera's 1972 ABC documentary comparing Letchworth with a facility in California. Rivera's TV cameras graphically portrayed the New York facility as "backward and cruel" where patients lived in "awful, dirty and overcrowded conditions, with a lack of clothing, bathing, and attention of their basic needs." Congressman Mario Biaggi, who accompanied Rivera, stated, "The worst possible conditions I've ever seen in my life".

Since its closure in 1996, many of the building at Letchworth decayed under the harsh winter and summer weather. Broken windows and doors have allowed animals to occupy some of the buildings, leaving waste. Paint peels from the walls, littering the floors with insulation and tiles fallen from the ceilings. In offices, floors counter tops, and desks are covered with records, many of them reveal personal health information of the patients. Some ghost hunters have reported spotting stacks of death certificates that are clearly legible.

Some of the grounds have been converted to the Veterans Memorial Park and Patriot Hills Golf Course. Eight buildings have been renovated and rented as commercial centers or private offices, but several structures remain in a state of slow decay. *No trespassing* signs are posted on buildings deemed unsafe for entry.

While it is easy, and legal, to enter buildings now dedicated to government offices or private commercial activity, few ghost hunters have gained entry to the abandoned buildings. In episode six of season seven, the cast of *Ghost Adventures* documented their 2011 investigation of the village. The show provides a graphic view of the abandoned buildings and fascinating yet disturbing vintage video that displays the deplorable conditions to which the patients were subjected in the final years of the institution's operations.

The Ghost Adventures team obtained some vague thermal images that may be paranormal, but two EVP stand-out as convincing evidence of ghostly activity. While investigating the morgue's body cabinet, Aaron Goodwin was told, "Shut up, you prick." Lead investigator Zak Bagans obtained a frightening EVP in a rough masculine voice that advised, "Pray to your god."

Local ghost investigators featured on the show revealed negative effects of their frequent visits to Letchworth that included a frightening voice emanating from their car's radio during a drive home after an investigation, and an admission that they had become addicted" to the place. Zak interpreted the admission as possible spirit attachment that created personal problems for the investigators.

Others who have explored the remnants of Letchworth have reported encounters with cells of cold air even in summer heat. Disembodied sounds of children laughing, crying, screaming, and calling for help have also been reported. A reported posted on the Internet described one investigator's ghostly encounter that resulted in her being pinned to floor, unable to move.

It is unknown how many patients died a Letchworth, but a small cemetery contains the remains of nearly a thousand patients. Located about 1.5 miles from the village, near the intersection of Camp Winaki Road and Call Hollow Road, the cemetery is marked with a stone tablet that contains the names of many buried there.

Access to the grounds of the former asylum is not restricted. Structures that remain in a state of decay are closed, naturally, and entry is considered trespassing. Some buildings are accessible because they are now used for pubic business such as the Kirkbride Hall, Stony Point Justice Court, and the Cornell University Cooperative Extension of Rockland County.

*   *   *   *

CHAPTER 22

ASYLUM THAT BECAME A MOVIE SET

Medfield State Hospital
45 Hospital Road
Medfield, Massachusetts 02052

Originally named Medfield Insane Asylum and dedicated to the humane treatment of the chronically insane, the grounds of this fascinating place are reputed to be the only abandoned psychiatric hospital in the US that is open to the public. While that is not entirely true, the grounds of this former asylum are open to joggers, dog-walkers, picnickers, and even ghost hunters, until sunset. Night access is prohibited and the restriction is enforced by guards and local police. Many visitors are initially surprised when they recognize certain locations on this campus despite not having had a previous visit. The recognition is due to Medfield serving as background for popular movies that include *The Box* (2009), the very scary *Shutter Island* (2010), and the X-Men film, the *New Mutants* (2020).

The grounds and abandoned buildings may evoke a sense of peace, but this asylum was the scene of at least three murders, 55 deaths from the 1918 Spanish Flu epidemic, untold numbers of patients treated with electro-convulsive shocks and insulin-shock therapy, and incarceration of several patients designated as criminally insane. In addition, the asylum's cemetery contains the remains of nearly 1,000 patients who were unclaimed by family members, leaving a pall of despondency felt by empaths.

Most of the development of this hospital occurred during its first twenty years. By 1920, most of its grounds had been developed, farms and shops established, and a power plant opened that supplied electricity to the entire campus of 1.3 square miles. At the greatest extent of development, the campus consisted of 58 buildings serving more than 2,000 patients with housing for some of the staff. Thirty-five buildings remain standing today, although entry is forbidden due to safety concerns.

In 1914, the name of the facility was changed to Medfield State Hospital to discard the stigma of a mental institution. Despite that altruistic objective, it has been estimated that about 60% of admitted patients did not have a mental illness. Many were developmentally delayed, retarded, or suffered from abuse or epilepsy.

Twenty years after its opening, like many asylums, Medfield became over-crowded, staffed with unqualified or otherwise incompetent attendants and nurses, and plagued by shortages of beds, clothing, and other supplies. By the 1930s, the place had a poor reputation and stories of patient abuse, mistreatment, and criminal behavior of both staff and patients began to surface. In 1902, 30-year old Deron McCormack was murdered by her room-mate. While strapped to her bed, unable to call for help or defend herself, Deron's room-mate bludgeoned her to death with a heavy iron object, probably a door stop. In 1916 Wesley Linton, an attendant at the hospital, plead guilty to assault, and beating and killing of a patient. He was removed from Medfield and sentenced to three years in the Dedham House of Correction.

Reports of heinous behavior at Medfield continued during the late 1980s and early 1990s, particularly after thirteen inmates from Bridgewater State Hospital for the Criminally Insane were relocated to the newly renovated, high-security "R" Building. One of these patients was "Blake," a mass murderer who had killed several members of his family. Another murderer was a boy named "Little Timmy" who, it is said, died at Medfield and haunts the basketball court enclosed by chain link fence.

In 2017, a movie crew spent several weeks on the campus filming scenes for the newest X-men film, *The New Mutants*. Several crew and actors reported. During meetings and media representatives, director Josh Boone mentioned that "weird" experiences were reported by several production staff. Many used phrases such as "totally creeped out," and "freaked by bizarre odors." Actor Henry Zaga said, "One element that was really present for me was the smell. It's something you can't really explain to someone. It just creeps into your soul."

While discussing the arcane history of the hospital, actor Maisie Williams (star of *Game of Thrones*) said, "There are all these spooky ghost stories going around and I think a lot of women were like lobotomized there." When filming at night ended, many actors demanded escorts from the various locations to the safety of waiting limos.

Despite several videos posted on YouTube that offer fascinating views of the Medfield campus, perspectives on its history and current state, and illicit scenes of the decay and disarray inside some of the buildings, there are no detailed reports of paranormal investigations. One investigator mentioned that the park-like environment, popular with dog-walkers and urban hikers, creates an atmosphere that is far from paranormal or even spooky. When I visited the place many years ago, I discovered several cold spots and other discreet locations that gave the impression gravity had increased 3-4 times, as if a force were pulling me downward. I inquired about underground tunnels that may have been used to facilitate movement between buildings, but guards and local historians had no verifiable information about such passageways. Even in afternoon sunlight, the campus was beautifully creepy, giving the clear impression that unseen beings were watching me while some, obscured by dirty windows, beckoned me to join them in the misery of a life without hope.

During the first decade of its operation, 520 patients who died at Medfield State Hospital were buried in Medfield's Vine Lake Cemetery. As the 1918 Spanish Flu epidemic swept through the region, the town of Medfield realized it needed every available grave site for its citizens. In one year, 17 residents of the town died of the flu. The hospital had a much higher death, with as many as 55 dying in one month. This prompted the hospital to open its own graveyard on 2.5 acres of land which was used until 1988. The cemetery is located on North Meadows Road, about one quarter mile east of the Charles River.

This small cemetery contains 841 graves that were, until 2005, marked only with a stone engraved with a number. The deceased were interred in this cemetery because their remains went unclaimed by family members. This has triggered speculation among paranormal investigators that ghosts of the dead may have remained at the burial site awaiting a caring relative.

In 2005, the Medfield State Hospital Cemetery Restoration Committee enlisted the help of local Boy Scouts to restore the grounds of the cemetery. Money was raised that supported research into the identity of each graveyard resident and the creation of granite grave markers engraved with names, and dates of birth and death. This information may prove useful to ghost hunters who visit this cemetery. Generally, EVP is more readily captured on audio recorders if the investigator questions a spirit by name, adding specific information such as ate of death.

Near the wrought iron gate stands monument engraved with a message from the dead to the living: "Remember us for we too have lived, loved and laughed."

*   *   *   *

CHAPTER 23

FOUR HUNDRED SUITCASES

Willard Asylum Museum
Romulus Historical Society
1371 County Road 132
Ovid, New York 14521

In 1995, weeks after the Willard Psychiatric Center closed, workers entered the attic and discovered a treasure trove of personal memorabilia in the form of more than 400 suitcases. These suitcases were confiscated from patients during the admission process and, owning to their presence in the attic, it is clear that their owners did not leave the hospital alive. Hence, the personal belongings of at least 400 patients remained forgotten in the attic until 1995.

Many suitcases contained photographs of family members, including parties and events, that may have been packed with clothing as emotional anchors intended to remind the mentally ill patient of happier times and pleasant situations that might be attained, once again, in the future. Some photographs pictured patients driving cars, playing sports, reading books, traveling and working at their jobs, offering rare insight into the pre-illness life that Willard's patients enjoyed.

Faces displayed in suitcase photographs in the Willard Asylum Museum evoke a sense of sadness that these people, despite successful employment, family and community connections, and personal accomplish-ments, fell into the dark hole of mental illness. Clearly, something happened that caused their lives to collapse. Maybe it was physical illness, loss of a loved one whose image was captured in the hundreds of photographs, sudden poverty, divorce, or some other catastrophic event most of us cannot imagine.

One of 400 suitcase discovered at Willard Asylum soon after it closed.

The contents of these suitcases also raise questions about reasons for committal to Willard Insane Asylum. Did the patient pack the suitcase or did a distressed family member? Why did they stay so long that they died in the asylum? And finally, why did psychiatric treatment fail to restore the life represented by the artifacts in these 400 suitcases?

Despite is altruistic mission and dedication of its founders, the first patients to enter Willard Asylum would have given any witness the impression that the place was about to be filled with the dregs of humanity plagued with mental and physical illness that could never be cured.

On October 13, 1869, a steamboat cruised north on Lake Seneca to Ovid Landing. One of the first to step ashore was Mary Rote. Described as deformed and demented, Mary was sent to Willard from an almshouse in Columbia County where, it was clear, she had been chained to a bed for many years, fed with a meager diet, and clothed with rags. Later that day, more patients arrived at the landing, restrained with irons and contained in small crates resembling chicken coops. Over the ensuing weeks, many more patients arrived at Willard's lakefront landing.

These unfortunate souls were gathered from New York State's almshouses because they could not work in the fields, orchards, or farms, or perform any other useful work that would support the almshouse community. Willard accepted these people because its staff of doctors believed they had new insight into mental illness and novel ideas for treatment. Grasping at the opportunity to be relieved of the burden of supporting the chronically insane, many almshouses sent patients to Willard. Within a few months of its opening, the asylums 250-bed capacity was exceeded, and over-crowding became a problem that persisted 150 years.

As the next decades passed, it was clear that Willard Asylum for the Insane had a low rate of successful treatment and a very large population of patients who would never leave.

The history of Willard is fascinating, but the perspective offered more than twenty years after its closing reveals an asylum on a slippery slope, destined for insurmountable problems that ultimately filled a cemetery with nearly 6,000 bodies.

Many of the buildings that became the Willard Asylum for the Chronically Insane were originally erected as a college in 1853. By 1861, the place was deserted as faculty and students enlisted in the Union Army. Facilities were enlarged in 1866 to include a huge central structure patterned after the Kirkbride philosophy for asylums with a central administration building, capped with a tall steeple, and two wings spreading outward designed to allow good light penetration and ventilation.

Some of the bodies buried in Willard's cemetery first passed through the morgue for autopsy.

In 1870, construction of detached buildings began, starting with Sunnycroft that contained eight 50-bed dormitories with accommodations for supervisory staff. In 1870, Edgemere was built. Eventually, Willard Asylum for the Chronically became known as Willard State Hospital and its patient census exceeded 2,000 in 1890, out-growing the facilities despite the construction of 70 buildings that included a Warden's house overlooking the dock on Lake Seneca, numerous dormitory style buildings to house both residents and staff, a morgue, a fire department, a nurse's station (now used as a daycare facility), a power station, gymnasium, chapel, and a movie theatre. The morgue still stands and houses several autopsy tables and cadaver drawers. Nearby, the crematorium still has that musty, dirty odor.

Eventually, the old model on which this Asylum was founded became obsolete. A nursing ratio than increased to one nurse to 150 patients signaled the end of the giant Kirkbride style institution. In 1995, the last patient left Willard, destined to a community based out-patient mental health program.

So, why would Willard asylum be haunted?

Some of the people who were incarcerated in this place suffered from the effects of electro-shock therapy, isolation and deprivation, and daily ice baths used to "calm" agitated patients. Of the 50,000 people admitted to Willard over its 150 years, about 25,000 died at the asylum.

Undoubtedly, many of the patients were not actually suffering from mental illness. Epileptics, high-functioning autistics, and others suffering from depression were admitted for "treatment" but the incarceration only made them angry and desperate for escape. Little has been reported of patient abuse, but it seems certain that many were mistreated.

Due to the severely limited access, no paranormal group has performed an investigation at Willard asylum. When pandemic restrictions are relaxed, and the Drug Treatment Center re-instates tours and general access, we may have some amazing stories of the ghost of lost souls that still wander the hallways of this asylum.

A short distance west of the asylum campus, on County Road 132, ghost hunters will find a 30-acrea cemetery that contains the remains of 5,776 graves. Opened in 1870 and used until 2000, the cemetery touches the shore of Lake Seneca at the spot where Mary Rote and the first patients of Willard Asylum stepped ashore in 1869. A sign marks the entrance as a gravel road conveys visitors to some very spooky ground. Cast iron markers, engraved with a number, mark some graves. Others – about thirty-eight – have headstones provided by the U.S. government inscribed with the names of Civil War veterans. The remaining graves are discernible only by a concrete disk embedded with a metal medallion engraved with a number.

Members of a local cemetery project have worked to locate graves and identify the deceased, but the ignominious burial of so many hapless people still distresses many visitors. One remarked, "Knowing that this is the final resting place of 5,776 people made me sick. It was disgraceful. I have never seen anything like it before."

Willard patients were interred here because no one claimed the body for burial elsewhere, or the family of the deceased had no money for transport and burial. It is certain that many ended up here because the family could not endure the shame of mental illness that would fall upon them if they stepped forward to claim the body.

The most famous resident of this cemetery is Lawrence Mochi (June 23, 1878-October 26, 1968). In effect, a celebrity among local history buffs, Mochi was admitted to Willard Asylum in1916 after suffering a head injury. It is said that, in his youth, he was an alcoholic yet he served in the Army, probably between 1898 and 1902. His involvement in an argument or fight caused his admission to a psychiatric hospital in New York City and from there, transfer to Willard where he remained until his death in 1968.

Apparently, Mochi was a well-behaved patient because by 1937 he was treated as a staff member and even allowed to live alone in a shack at the cemetery where he was employed as a grave digger, using only a pick and shovel. He also assisted other staff in construction of coffins and preparation of bodies for burial. By 1951, Mochi had dug more than 900 graves, six feet deep and 60 to a row. In his later years his pace slowed but he is credited with digging 1,500 graves and maintaining the graveyard. It has been reported that, in the final years of his life, Mochi showed no signs of mental illness and he took no medication.

Because Lawrence Mochi was officially a patient at the asylum, his burial site was marked only with a number, according to state law. With the passage of only a few years, his shack was dismantled and the location of his grave forgotten.

In 2017, members of the Willard Cemetery Memorial Project discovered Mochi's burial site in grave 45, row 2. The state of New York would not permit members to place a headstone containing his name, but they inserted a metal rod in the ground and hung a red lantern as a kind of monument.

The Willard grave digger has achieved a kind of notoriety that attracts historians and ghost hunters. I found no reports of paranormal activity at this cemetery attributed to Mochi, but in other cemeteries I discovered the grave diggers tend to remain devoted to the job after death. So, an investigation specifically aimed at Mochi may be productive and verify his devotion to the cemetery.

Willard gravedigger and patient, Lawrence Mochi.

Because the grounds of the old asylum now comprise the Drug Treatment Campus (DTC), access is severely restricted. The DTC opens some of the historic buildings to visitors only one day each year and entry is permitted only in highly organized and supervised groups of 25 to 40 people. The three-hour walking tour is governed closely by docents, leaving no chance for breaking away from the group for a little personal time with Willard's ghosts.

There has never been a website offering information about tours. The best source of information may be https://homeinthefingerlakes.com/willard-tour-cemetery/.

* * * *

CHAPTER 24

HOME OF THE LOBOTOMY

Remains of Danvers State Hospital
1101 Kirkbride Drive
Danvers, MA 01923

The architecture is beautifully spooky. A tall central tower, spires, sharply angled roof lines, red brick exterior, gables, and tall windows capped with granite remain as original elements of the former administration building and wards designated G and D of the Kirkbride Plan asylum built in 1874. These exterior features were spared when the interior, and most of the hospital campus, was gutted in 2006. The new interior structure now serves as a professional office building while condominiums and apartments now cover the 500 acres where more than forty buildings once comprised the hospital campus.

Originally designed to house 450 patients, by 1885 a patient population of nearly 800 created severe overcrowding. By 1901, the population exceeded 1,000 leading to the addition of 500 beds in 1926. As the number of patients approached 2,000 in 1927, the superintendent of the hospital, Dr. Clarence Bonner, believed greater use of restraints was required, including "special garments," meaning straight-jackets, with isolation. The large number of patients also provided subjects for several experimental treatments.

By the 1930s, the quality of care had deteriorated as the inadequate staff struggled to control the massive number of patients with more rigorous means such as lobotomy and electric shock therapy. Due to staff shortages, neglected patients, many of them medicated with tranquilizing drugs, reportedly walked the hallways naked while others were left in filthy beds for several days without nursing care. As the annual death rate increased and the massive structure deteriorated, patients were moved to other facilities and the hospital closed in 1991.

The newly renovated and repurposed Danvers State Hospital.

It is said that tunnels that once connected many of the hospital's buildings remain together with other remnants of the lunatic asylum used in the renovation of the main building including a great deal of wood, door hinges and knobs, and threshold hardware. Perhaps these elements retain or attract ghosts from the dark days of this institution.

Soon after the hospital's closure, ghost hunters and urban explorers reported intense paranormal phenomena including doors that opened and closed by unseen hands, the sound of footsteps on floors and stairs, and even full-bodied apparitions of patients wandering about, screaming. Sensitives perceived feelings of sadness and despair, and empaths became ill.

Since renovation of the administration building there has been much speculation about the persistence of paranormal activity. Ghost hunters using psychic methods may perceive eerie vibes while walking the grounds or touching the exterior walls of the main building, but the old hospital's two cemeteries may be a better place to look for spirits of the mentally ill. Stone markers, engraved with the patient's number, stand as stark memorials to 770 people who suffered and died at Danvers hospital.

The Danvers lunatic asylum cemetery may be found by walking southeasterly on Kirkbride Drive. Pass the small parking lot and the over-look plaza to the gravel path that leads down the hill, though the trees, to the cemetery. To reach the hospital's Middleton cemetery, park at the intersection of Gregory Street and Middleton Road, in Middleton. Follow the path to the cemetery which is enclosed by a fence and shaded by several trees.

*   *   *   *

CHAPTER 25

Other Hot Spots to Investigate

Locations included in this chapter have very limited access, or no access at the time this book was published. These fascinating mental health facilitates may soon become fully accessible and provide ghost hunters with opportunities to be among the first to investigation them. Watch for the asylums listed in this chapter to become hot spots for paranormal investigators in the near future.

The Ridges – Athens Lunatic Asylum
Now: the Kennedy Museum of Art
   of the Ohio University
24 West State Street
Athens, OH 45701
740-592-2280

Constructed in 1874 and closed in 1993, the Athens Lunatic Asylum served Civil War veterans suffering from PTSD, mentally ill and retarded children, and violent criminals. Like many facilities of the era, initial treatments were humane, following the philosophy of contemporary mental health advocates such as Dorothea Dix and Dr. Thomas Kirkbride. In fact, the massive hospital was designed and operated according to the Kirkbride Plan and included farms, orchards, a water supply system and shops intended to make the place nearly self-sufficient.

Known as The Ridges, a moniker not attached to the place until 1984, over-crowding became a critical issue by 1900 and the quality of treatment declined. By 1950, the patient population reached nearly 2,000 housed in a campus of 78 buildings sitting on 1,019 acres. Gruesome treatments became standard at this asylum, including lobotomies, isolation devices such as bed restraints and straight jackets, iced water baths, and psychotropic drugs.

In a room adjacent to the museum's entrance, visitors may view vintage photographs from the asylum's history and several artifacts including a lobotomy pick, reportedly used on as many as twenty patients in a single day, and an electro-convulsive shock machine. The exhibit also includes oral histories by doctors, patients, and their families.

The creepiest feature of the old asylum is an indelible stain on the attic floor created by a tragic event in December of 1979. Patient Margaret Shilling was enjoying a game of hide-and-seek and chose to hide in attic beyond the view of supervising nurses. Apparently, when the game ended, the attic door was locked, leaving Margaret in a dark, unheated space. A frantic search was staged that ended when supervisors concluded she had somehow left the facility.

It wasn't until January that her body was discovered. Today, an imprint of her body, clothes, and hair are clearly visible on the floor despite decades of cleaning. Many believe her ghost still wanders the hallways of this old asylum and may be responsible for the residual imprint of her body on the attic floor.

Three cemeteries contain the graves of 1,930 former patients of The Ridges Asylum. Markers at 1,659 graves are engraved only with a number. Many ghost hunters believe the anonymous graves have led to a lot of paranormal activity by spirits who desire recognition of their final resting place. Some visitors have reported screaming and humanoid shadows.

Today, the Ridges is part of Ohio University and houses the Kennedy Museum of Art, an auditorium and offices, classrooms, and storage facilities.

A stain created by the decomposition of the body
of Margaret Shilling

Babcock Building
The Old South Carolina State Hospital
Pickens Street at Elmwood Avenue
Columbia, South Carolina 29201

Construction of the South Carolina Lunatic Asylum started in 1822 and spanned five years. Housed in the Mills Building, named for its designer, Robert Mills, the asylum admitted its first patient in 1828. Initially, only white people were admitted, although some African Americans (including slaves) were treated in the hospital before 1848, when the State formally authorized admission of Black people.

Construction of another large hospital building – the Babcock Building - started in1858 but was stalled when designer George E. Walker died before completing the south wing. Architect Samuel Sloan took over the project and finished the main building despite several delays caused by the onset of the Civil War. The hospital campus was finally completed in 1885 with the addition of several out-buildings that housed a mattress factory, carpenter shop, bakery, and even an ice cream plant.

Unlike the Mills Building, construction of this asylum followed the Kirkbride Plan that included impressive architectural features, a "bat-wing" footprint, long hallways, tall ceilings, and large windows that provided sunlight and good ventilation. By 1900, the asylum population reached 1,000. In 1950, about 5,000 patients were housed in the Babcock and Mills buildings while some female patients were placed in small "cottages."

Ongoing issues with staffing, funding, and patient conditions persisted into the 20th century, ultimately leading to closure of the campus to in-patient treatment in 1996 and closure as a mental health facility in 2015.

Ghost hunters who were able to enter the Babcock Building prior to a devastating fire in 2020, reported disembodied sobbing and screams, and the muted chatter of spirits speaking incoherently. The sounds of hospital equipment, such as gurneys and wheelchairs, moving about were also detected throughout the building. EVP were frequently captured, and dowsing rods were very active. I found no reports of apparitions, but during my visit, I spotted a humanoid shadow moving along a wall in the basement. The rough brick walls of the catacomb-like rooms and passageways obscured the detail of this shadow, but it appeared as a tall and thin person, reaching out with a long arm.

Several images of the interior of the Babcock Building, before the fire of 2020, may be viewed online that evoke a deep sense of creepiness. Visit: amyheiden.com/

Babcock-building. Graffiti, peeling paint and wall painter, remnants of soiled carpets, broken windows with iron bars still in place, exposed pipes and wires, and scattered trash left by vandals and squatters obscure ornate architectural elements that reflected the altruistic aims the asylum's founders and most of the staff.

Many patients were treated with lobotomy and restraint devices in addition to a baseline level of care that was miserable due to over-crowding, staff neglect, and personal abuse that fostered hopeless and severe depression. Retired nurses who spoke out years after the asylum closed have recounted stories of patient suicides, patient attacks on staff, electroshock therapy without sedation, and aggravation of mental illness that virtually eliminated any chance of improvement or recovery.

The old building has suffered two major fires, the first on December 13, 2018, when the building's roof caught fire causing $400,000 in damage. On September 12, 2020, another fire caused the building's dome to collapse and gutted the interior. At the time of this book's publication, reconstruction and renovation are underway with a completion target date in 2022.

The current plan is to divide the main building of the former asylum into apartments and offices. Ghost hunters anticipate a greater frequency of paranormal activity created by the fire and renovation. This would be a hot spot for investigations when the building reopens.

St. Vincent's Asylum
3500 NE 23rd Street
Oklahoma City, OK 73121

Opened in 1945, St. Vincent's Asylum is one of the newest haunted asylums in the US. Its mid-century style brick construction, with long, sleek lines, make the place look like an office building. Upgrades in 1953 kept the building functional as the patient population grew until closure in the early 1980s leaving a dark and miserable history, and several angry ghosts.

The building is not open to visitors, but some brave souls have ventured inside and captured some very creepy photographs of its interior that may be viewed at www.abandonedok.com.

St. Vincent's started as a mental asylum operated by a Catholic order, the Brothers of Mercy. Despite its religious philosophy and natural assumption of compassionate care and protection, bad things started happening about 1960. A nurse was found guilty of suffocating two patients. No public explication was offered as the incident seemed to be managed in a way that limited publicity.

In the 1980s, Father Frank Dolan, the priest who supervised the asylum, changed the focus of care to drug rehabilitation. While serving an addicted population, Father Frank was arrested for soliciting prostitution. This may have been the tip of the iceberg of Father Frank's shady side, because he was murdered on the property, allegedly by patients he was trying to help. There are rumors of other strange and tragic events at St. Vincent's that ultimately led to its closure in the late 1980s.

The abandoned asylum is believed to be haunted by the ghost of Father Frank and the patients murdered by a nurse. Other tortured spirits roam the place including a teenaged boy who died of drug over-dose, and a young woman who may have been raped in the bathroom on the ground floor of the old section of the building.

Some paranormal investigators believe the place harbors a demonic entity that may have caused murderous behavior in nurses and patients.

Photographs that may be viewed online reveal a very creepy place that highlight the miserable history of St. Vincent's. Graffiti, bathrooms covered with rust and dusty scum, broken mirrors and windows, and a naked doll coated with red candle wax evoked a sense of dread and sadness in those who were able to enter the building. Scattered furniture and scrubs once worn by hospital staff are stained with a substance that may be blood.

Do not enter the asylum without explicit permission. It sits on private property and trespassers will be cited by police.

Zelda Fitzgerald's Abandoned Sanatorium
7 Craig House Lane
Beacon, New York, 12508

Constructed in 1859 for General Joseph Howland, who later served in the Civil War, this spectacular Gothic mansion was known as Tioranda until 1915 when it became America's first private psychiatric hospital. Doctor Clarence and his son, Jonathan, renamed the mansion Craig House and operated the hospital with "progressive attitudes" that included intensive talk therapy, fine dining experiences, and recreational activities such as golf, skiing, and painting. Basically, Craig House was a psychiatric spa for the rich and famous.

Zelda Fitzgerald spent some time at Craig House in 1934 after her husband, novelist F. Scott Fitzgerald moved her from the Phipps Clinic, a part of Johns Hopkins in Baltimore. Apparently she liked the place because she wrote to Scott, "there is everything on Earth available and I have a little room to paint in with a window higher than my head the way I like windows to be."

She also loved playing golf with Dr. Slocum, but the $750 per month fee was a financial stress Scott could not handle. In 1938, he moved Zelda to Highland Hospital in North Carolina here she died in 1948 (see chapter 17).

Despite its beautiful and serene 60 acres of park-like grounds, several tragedies occurred at Craig House. Actor Henry Fonda's wife, Frances Seymour, mother of actress Jane Fonda, committed suicide in 1942, in one of the turrets, by cutting her throat with a razor. Rosemary Kennedy (1918-2005), elder sister of President John F. Kennedy and Senators Robert F. and Ted Kennedy, was sent here in November of 1941 for treatment of her violent mood swings and seizure. At the age of 23, she was treated with lobotomy leaving her with the mental capacity of a two year old child.

The hospital closed its doors until 1999, leaving records of patients sealed. There are no rumors of patient abuse that are so prevalent at public asylums, but many speculate that several patients died on the premises or other portions of the large estate such as the hat factory and school house that also served as a church.

Even after the closure of Craig House, tragedies continued. In 2013, ten years after he purchased the old mansion, hedge fund manager Robert Wilson (1926-2013) suffered a stroke and jumped out the window of his New Your

City apartment. In that same year, the estate's administration building across the street was destroyed by fire.

Craig House sat abandoned for years before an investment group purchased the estate and developed plans to create a 15-room boutique hotel in the old asylum and 200 additional rooms in new construction. They proposed construction of a Nordic spa, incorporating remnants of the school house, a music studio, conference center, and 20 suite along the banks of the Hudson River.

When this place opens in 2023 it would provide ghost hunters with a fantastic opportunity to book a room and spend a weekend in a historic asylum.

Harlem Valley Psychiatric Center
181 Hutchinson Avenue
Wingdale, NY 12594

Harlem Valley State Hospital opened in 1924 and during its 70 years of operation, its doctors treated more than 5,000 patients on a campus composed of eighty building covering 900 acres. Facilities included a golf course, bowling alley, baseball field, bakery, and a dairy farm that supplied an in-house ice cream parlor.

The place also had treatment rooms for electro-coOnvulsive shock therapy, insulin coma therapy, and operating rooms for lobotomy procedures. In fact, in the 1940s, the Harlem Valley Psychiatric Center was the preeminent institution for frontal lobotomy in the state of New York.

For nearly twenty years the place sat abandoned, deteriorating rapidly in the climate of up-state New York. As the place took on a creepier appearance, ghost stories started to circulate in the region despite fences and security guards intended to keep curious urban explorers, and ghost hunters from entering the campus.

In 2013, the property was purchase by a develop-ment company with the intention of creating an evangelical Christian college. Occupational safety issues stalled the project as asbestos and lead removal procedures were found to be in violation of standards.

Inspired by a few reports from people who have entered the property, many paranormal investigators believe this place is haunted. Some of these reports may be found at hauntedearthghostvideos.blogspot.com.

In 2011, Jeremy Brown of Hiddenhometown.com was given permission to enter the ruins of the Harlem Valley Psychiatric Center. He reported that, "There is undoubtedly a presence of sorts inside those buildings. There's a heavy feeling of sadness that hangs over every room, a great sense of loneliness and despair. In certain places, like the padded cells, it was almost stifling."

Other reports include lights flashing in structures in which there is no electricity, the sounds of several dogs in the basement, and bruises found on the arms of ghost hunters.

Two cemeteries remain as monuments to those who died at Harlem Valley Psychiatric Hospital. The Eastern gate of Haven Cemetery is east of the town and requires a 2-mile hike. The Western gate of Haven Cemetery is a short distance west of Wingdale and easily accessed from Old Pawling Road, near the intersection with West Dover Road.

When renovation of the property is completed, access to remnants of the old asylum will be available for exciting ghost investigations.

Sonoma Developmental Center
15000 Arnold Dr.
Eldridge, CA 95431
Public Information: 707) 938-6143

In 1884, the state of California purchased land in the picturesque Sonoma Valley and later relocated schools for children with developmental disabilities from Vallejo and Santa Clara to the new facility that became known as the Sonoma Developmental Center (SDC). Opened in 1890 and designed according to the Kirkbride Plan, the wards, schools, and treatment rooms served 450 residents by the end of the century.

Like many asylums of the era, patients, or "clients" as SDC residents were called, worked in the orchards and farms, on maintenance of facilities, and performed other tasks as part of therapy. Many clients suffered from conditions that created severe musculo-skeletal disabilities without affecting the mind.

In 1909, involuntary sterilization was legalized in California and juvenile courts began sending large numbers of "defective delinquents" to the center. It is estimated at between 1909 and 1952, more than 5,000 men and women were involuntarily sterilized at this facility.

Other treatments, now considered inhuman, were routinely used at SDC including exposure to high doses of radiation. As many as 16,000 children were used in various radiation experiments described as "treatment." Between 1955 and 1960, a federally funded study of the effects of radiation on cerebral palsy was conducted on 1,100 children. Many received repeated doses and died of radiation poisoning.

Stories about radiation at SDC include survivors of the infamous Philadelphia Experiment conducted at the Philadelphia Naval Shipyard on October 28, 1943. Based on Alfred Einstein's Unified Field Theory, the Navy combined forces of electro-magnetism and gravity to bend light around a destroyer escort, the USS Eldridge, to render it invisible to German naval forces. Some witnesses claim the ship "disappeared" briefly only to reappear with some crew members embedded in the walls and deck, and others severely disoriented. A reliable source informed me that as many as seventeen crew members were transported to SDC and isolated in the main building for medical observation. Deeply disturbed, emotionally and mentally, all crew members eventually died at SDC. Local urban legends include unsubstantiated reports by former SDC staff members who claim several nurses and doctors became ill due to frequent contact with the naval crew.

Ghost hunters and conspiracy theorists fascinated by the Philadelphia Experiment have not yet gained access to the main building. There is no indication of residual radiation anywhere at SDC, but the spooky main building still attracts a lot of attention.

Southwest of the main campus, on Orchard Road (a short distance after the sharp right curve), a small cemetery contains the remains of 1403 unclaimed children and two employees. The last burial took place on December 9, 1939. Between 1940 and 1960, the ashes of 500 cremated clients were placed in a vault.

The main building at SDC remains inaccessible
to ghost hunters but the cemetery is open.

A wrought-iron gate, supported by stone pillars, opens to the cemetery that spreads over a grassy hillside. A plaque mounted on one of the pillars proclaims, "We remember you," evoking a sense of sadness. Visitors are also affected by a lone statue of a guardian angel that appears to be looking after the graves of the many children who were buried, unclaimed by their families. Graves are marked only by a concrete disk engraved with a number.

Sensitives feel the sadness of this place but, beyond this unavoidable emotion, many feel the tug of little hands on their jacket or hair. Some have reported a child's laugh and sobbing. Orbs are often captured by digital cameras and dowsing roads are very active.

In the early 1980s, several hundred surplus acres of SDC property were deeded to the adjacent Jack London State Park. The SDC facility closed in 2018 but many buildings remain standing that may soon become accessible to ghost hunters.

Unmarked Graves
Napa State Hospital
2100 Napa Vallejo Hwy
Napa, CA 94558
707-253-5000

While visiting the Napa Valley for wine tasting, ghost hunters may want to stop at Napa State Hospital to visit a vast graveyard with no headstones or other markers. This is still a working hospital for patients with mental illness, including nearly 600 who were found not guilty of a crime by reason of insanity and another 300 who were deemed incompetent to stand trial. The grounds are accessible to respectful visitors, including a cemetery that has attracted a lot of attention from historians and ghost hunters.

In 1872, the State of California purchased 192 acres from rancher Don Cayetano Juárez (1809-1883) and constructed a massive insane asylum that opened on 1875. The facility was modeled after the Kirkbride Plan with a "bat wing" footprint, several spires, and a central bell tower standing 150 feet above the ground. Built to accommodate 600 patients, by 1890 the in-patient population exceeded 1,300. Expansion of the wards and treatment facilities continued over many years, resulting in several "cottages" designed to accommodate twenty-six patients but often over-crowded with as many as seventy-five. The expansive property included a dairy farm and poultry ranches, a vegetable garden, and fruit orchards in addition to its own power plant and water supply. Treatments routinely used at Napa State Hospital included lobotomy, hydrotherapy in iced water, straight jackets, padded cells, and electro-convulsive shock therapy.

From 1875 to 1924, the hospital's cemetery was filled with 4,368 unclaimed bodies. Some graves once had wooden markers, but no monuments remain today. The cemetery can be found by locating the barn and calf pens on Madrone Drive, east of the main hospital. These structures sit over the burial ground, adding to the sad and ignominious fate of those interned here.

Visiting this place at night is not a good idea. Daytime ghost hunters have detected some strange phenomena including unexplained cold "cells" in stagnant air and a sensation of variable or shifting gravity, giving sensitives the impression of being pulled downward. Dowsing rods can be very active here, as well. Electro-magnetic field detectors register anomalies in many locations.

* * * *

CHAPTER 26

A FINAL WORD

Actually, a number of words are important to keep in mind when investigating asylums.

Respect for boundaries: Some of the places included in this book are still operating as hospitals or other health care entities. Often newer buildings on a campus are in use for patient care while older structures are open as museums, historic sites, or open for tours by special arrangement. Respect the limits implicit in the access that is granted. Do not enter areas currently in use as out-patient or in-patient treatment areas.

Do not trespass: Each year many ghost hunters are arrested for illegal entry. Even if a structure appears completely abandoned and entry is easy, do not yield to your curiosity and enter without explicit permission to do so.

Compassion: Despite the reality of bodily death, most ethical ghost hunters demonstrate compassion for the dead, especially those who were tortured by heinous treatment and abuse, and the misery of mental illness. Do not try to entice spirit manifestation or provoke spirits by insults, lies, teasing, mimicking a mental illness, or claiming you are a doctor or nurse.

Protection: Follow the guidelines for protection against malevolent spirits presented in Chapter 3. In particular, avoid drugs or alcohol during the 12-24 hours prior to your visit to a haunted asylum. Spirits that are not malevolent may attach to ghost hunters simply because of the vulnerability created by these substances.

ETHICS AND STANDARDS

There is no governing body that regulates ghost hunters and the practice of paranormal investigation. That is really no surprise because ghost hunters tend to be staunchly independent people who travel their own path, practice their craft without regard to the distraction of contrary opinions or advice of others, and see the world according to their own talents, skills, and experiences. Moreover, most paranormal investigators don't feel they need the support or representation of a formal association nor do they believe in the value of certification.

As a consequence of all of that, there is no clear, authoritative statement about standards and ethics of psychic practice particularly as it relates to relationships with clients or organization that may grant access for places as such haunted asylums.

You should conduct your investigation with due consideration of the following concerns;

Ownership of Evidence: Ownership of evidence, which may be your written report or an audio or video recording made during an investigation for a client, is seldom an issue when paranormal investigative services are performed for the occupant of a private residence. In fact, most clients don't give the issue any thought. Evidence is looked upon as answers to perplexing questions, not as a potential source of monetary gain or basis of a legal dispute.

Both of those concerns may arise, however, when the client, or entity granting permission for you to investigate, is a government agency that has authority over a public service housed in a historic building. Ownership of evidence becomes a concern because these entities usually wish to avoid any publicity may create doubts in the minds of local citizens about the seriousness with which they are managed. Unfortunately, many people may believe that a government official must be mentally unstable or easily gullible if he or she is associated with a conclusion publicized by a ghost hunter that a hospital, out-patient treatment facility, or other public entity is haunted.

The best policy for a ghost investigator is to specify, on your Website or in a document you give to the client, that you retain ownership and copyright of all material derived from any research, interview, surveillance, or other source.

Release of Information: Agreements between a client and a paranormal investigator concerning the release of information may be complex because of the variety of information, variety of outlets for dissemination of information, lack of control of information once it is released, and the potential for negative effects that create problems for the client, owner of the property, and the persons who conducted the investigation.

Nonetheless, it is vital that some agreement be reached regarding the degree to which information may be released in order to safeguard the personal identity of the client or others, prevent undesired notoriety of the investigation site, and avoid attracting other investigators to the site who may interfere with your future investigations.

Paranormal investigation is not a science. While many verifiable facts may be uncovered in the course of an investigation, paranormal investigators should not guarantee, or otherwise affirm, the accuracy of findings or validity of evidence derived from a psychic investigation or obtained from audio recording, imaging, or other devices.

No guarantee should be made that banishing procedures will be successful in reducing or eliminating paranormal activity at a location. While every effort will be made to serve the client, due to the unpredictable nature of paranormal activity, there is no guarantee that all of the client's concerns or needs can be met with complete satisfaction.

Do not reveal names of people you may interview, such as former inmates of an asylum or staff members, without explicit permission to do so.

Be careful, ethical, and well-researched. Asylums are truly unique venues for ghost hunters where ghostly encounters are nearly guaranteed.

*   *   *   *